FIRST RIGHTS

A Guide to Legal Rights for Young People

Maggie Rae, Patricia Hewitt and Barry Hugill

Illustrations by Corinne Pearlman

National Council for Civil Liberties 1979

NCCL Know Your Rights Handbooks

Series editors Patricia Hewitt and Charles Foster

1. **Race Relations Guide** published 1978 50p
2. **Your Rights at Work** published 1978 70p
3. **First Rights — a guide to legal rights for young people** published 1979 80p

In preparation
Prisoners' Rights

For further details of these and all other NCCL publications please write to NCCL, 186 Kings Cross Road, London WC1X 9DE.

Note

The law is different in Scotland and Northern Ireland. This book only deals with England and Wales. On page 107, we give some useful books and addresses of organisations which can help. Although all details in this book are correct at the time of going to press the law on certain points is subject to change.

Acknowledgements

The authors would like to express their heartfelt thanks to all those who have helped in the preparation of this book and especially Jenny Levin, Tess Gill, Joe Gill, Tom Gill, Larry Grant, Anna Coote and Charles Foster.

ISBN 0 901108 76 6 (paperback) 0 901108 82 0 (cased)

PRINTED IN GREAT BRITAIN
by the Russell Press, Nottingham

CONTENTS

The **National Council for Civil Liberties** has campaigned since 1934 to defend and extend freedom of speech and expression, and to protect the rights of individuals and minorities to equal treatment under just laws. NCCL advises people on their rights; takes cases to courts and tribunals; lobbies Parliament and Government through an all-party Parliamentary Civil Liberties Group; publishes pamphlets about people's rights; and organises campaigns for law reforms. Funded solely by subscriptions and donations, NCCL is the largest independent organisation working for human rights in the United Kingdom.

You can get further details of individual membership or affiliation by organisations or groups from NCCL, 186 Kings Cross Road, London WC1X 9DE.

INTRODUCTION

Attitudes towards childhood and youth have changed dramatically over the centuries. In medieval and Tudor Britain, for instance, children and young people worked alongside their parents in the fields or were apprenticed at an early age to learn a craft, while boys from upper-class families were sent away to court for their training.

The idea of 'childhood' as a state entirely different from adulthood, demanding widespread special protection and carrying few if any responsibilities was developed later, initially in wealthier families who could afford not to have their young people working. In working-class families, of course, economic demands meant that children had to earn their living from a very early age and, up until only 100 years ago, children and teenagers were to be found working in the mines, in factories, as chimney-sweeps and on the streets.

In 1819, a law was passed preventing children under nine from working in mines or factories. In 1874, a minimum age of ten was set for most jobs. In addition to the rules governing the employment of school-students, the Factories Acts place restrictions on the hours worked by women and by young people up to the age of 18.

The 1918 Education Act established compulsory education up to the age of 14; the school-leaving age was lifted to 15 in 1947 and again to 16 in 1972. Raising the school-leaving age was designed to improve educational opportunities, particularly for less well-off children; it also had the effect of delaying further the arrival of legal adulthood.

This guide sets out to explain, as clearly and practically as possible, the way the law treats young people. But laws change, as social conditions change, and the present state of the law is not fixed. Different countries have different rules about what age you can leave school, consent to a sexual relationship, get married, and so on. The law in Britain says that you can marry at 16 with your parents' consent: but that doesn't mean it's right for you, as an individual, to marry at that age. We can't make decisions for you, and this guide cannot tell you what to do or give you advice on personal problems. But we do believe that, in order for you to make decisions about your own life, you need the fullest possible information about how the law will affect you. We hope you'll be able to discuss your own situation, and the legal position, with sympathetic adults. But if you're isolated, we suggest you contact one of the organisations listed on pages 107-12 and at the end of each chapter of this guide.

This guide is published as part of NCCL's contribution to the International Year of the child. NCCL is also carrying out a study of children and young people in institutions.

We would be grateful for any comments, suggestions or criticisms you have, so that we can take them into account when this guide is reprinted.

Patricia Hewitt
General Secretary, NCCL

July 1979

1

YOU AND YOUR FAMILY

This chapter covers:

Courts

In this chapter, we sometimes mention 'the court' which may be asked to make a decision about you and your family. There are a number of courts which can be involved in family matters: for instance, the magistrates' court deals with couples who are separated and who disagree about how much maintenance should be paid or where the children should live. The divorce courts handle matters where people are getting divorced and, again, may have to make a decision about where the children should live. In rare cases, a child may be made a 'ward of court' (for instance, to prevent one parent taking the child out of the country), and this would be dealt with by the High Court. It would be a good idea to have one 'family court' to deal with most of these matters, but the government has refused the plan on the grounds that it would cost too much.

Living with your parents

Until you are 18, you are still a 'minor' and the law treats you as incapable of looking after yourself on your own and making all your own decisions. Of course, as you get older, you are more able to decide things for yourself — particularly if you start work at 16 and support yourself. But while you are under 18, the law generally assumes that you are under the control of an adult or adults — usually your parents.

Your parents — or whichever adults have charge of you — are said to have *custody* of you. In practice, this means they have the legal right to decide where you go to school, what you wear, how much pocket-money you get, how you are punished and so on. If your parents do not look after you properly, the courts can give

She says she wants to leave home, but I know she doesn't mean it.

DOCTOR

The law says your parents have custody of you whilst you are under 18.

custody to someone else, or the local authority can take you into *care* (this is explained in chapter 3).

If your parents were not married when you were born, and have not married since, then you are said to be 'illegitimate' — although the law makes very little distinction now between an 'illegitimate' and

8

a 'legitimate' child, and social prejudices are also breaking down. The law says that the mother has custody of an illegitimate child: the father has no automatic right to have custody of the child, although he can try to persuade a court to grant him custody (see page 12 for more on this).

Who pays for your keep

Your parents are responsible for maintaining you until you are 18. This applies even though they may not have custody of you. For instance, if you are living with your mother, your father still has to contribute towards your upkeep. If you are in the care of the local authority, the same applies and the court can order your parents to pay maintenance to the local authority for you.

If you get married before you reach the age of 18, then your parents are no longer responsible for maintaining you.

Neglect

If your parents fail to look after you properly or ill-treat you, a court can order that someone else should have custody of you. Your parents can be prosecuted for treating you cruelly or damaging your health. Alternatively, the local authority can decide to take you into care (see chapter 3). If you feel that you are being ill-treated by your parents, you can get advice and help from your local social services department, or from a friendly teacher or a lawyer (for instance, at a local law centre). It's best to seek advice rather than run away.

Your name

If your parents were married when you were born, then you were probably given your father's surname. If your parents separate and your mother wants to change your surname, she has to get your father's consent first. If your parents weren't married when you were born, then you will probably have been given your mother's surname – unless your mother decided that she wanted you to have your father's surname and allowed it to be put on your birth certificate.

Until you are 16, you cannot change your name without your parents' consent (or your mother's consent if you are illegitimate). Once you are 16, you must give your consent if your parents want to change your name (for instance, if your mother is divorced from your father and wants you to take the name of her new husband). Once you are 18, you can change your name without getting your parents' agreement. You can do this quite simply, just by using whatever name you like: or you can swear a statutory declaration or change your name by deed poll (go to a solicitor for this). But you can't have your birth certificate changed.

Citizenship and nationality

If you were born in the United Kingdom or one of the colonies (e.g. Gibraltar, Hong Kong or the Falkland Islands), then you are a United Kingdom citizen, whatever citizenship your parents had (unless your parents were diplomats from another country, in which case you won't get UK citizenship by being born here). If you were born abroad, then you will only be automatically entitled to UK citizenship if your father was a UK citizen and was married to your mother. But your mother can apply for you to have UK citizenship even if your father was a citizen of a foreign country. NCCL wants to see the law changed so that citizenship can be inherited through either the father or the mother.

Religion

You can't stop your parents making you a member of any particular faith or going through formal ceremonies such as baptism. Your parents can insist on you having religious instruction if you live at home, and you have no legal right to prevent this. It is also possible for one of your parents to alter your religion without your consent – for instance if there is a dispute about which religion you should take, or if your parents divorce – although the court can take your views into account if they think you are old enough. The court may also stop you being brought up in a particular religion if they think this would be bad for you.

If you are going to a state school, the law says you should have religious instruction unless your parents withdraw you from these classes. You have no right yourself to withdraw from religious instruction, but, if you want to, you can ask your parents to withdraw you.

Medical treatment

Normally, your parents will arrange for you to see the doctor if you are ill or need a check-up. If you have to go to hospital, they will sign the consent form saying that you can have an operation.

In theory, you have to be 16 before you can choose your own doctor, consent to medical treatment or insist on the doctor keeping secret what you tell him or her. But many doctors will treat younger people in confidence, particularly on contraceptive matters (see page 64). On pages 69-70 we list some organisations which may help if you feel you can't talk to your parents or family doctor.

medical, surgical or dental treatment. A parent or guardian has to sign the consent form for you (or a social worker if you have been taken into care). Once you have reached 16, you can consent to treatment yourself − but your parent or guardian also has the right to consent on your behalf until you are 18.

The law says that a girl aged under 16 needs the consent of a parent to have contraceptive treatment − for instance, to get the pill prescribed or have a coil fitted − or to have an abortion. In practice, parental consent is often not obtained (see page 64 for more on this). In theory, parents could force an abortion on a girl aged under 16 even though she did not want it, although doctors have refused to carry out the operation in such circumstances.

Where it is felt that parents are consenting to medical treatment which is not in the child's best interests, it is possible to stop the treatment by having the child made a 'ward of court' − which means that the court takes over the legal powers of the parents. For instance, an educational psychologist took legal proceedings in 1975 to prevent a handicapped 11-year-old girl being sterilized: the girl was made a ward of court and the court decided that the operation was unnecessary and refused its consent.

Travelling and getting a passport

You can travel with either of your parents on their passports. If you need a passport of your own, your parents have to apply for it for you. Once you reach 18, you can get your own passport without your parents' consent. If you are going abroad on a school trip, the school will probably get a group passport for all of you. On some day-trips to Europe you don't need a passport at all.

If you were born abroad, or if your parents are not UK citizens, then you may have a passport from a different country. But your citizenship could change if, for instance, you were born in a country which was then a United Kingdom colony and which later became independent. People born in St Lucia and Jamaica, for instance, while those countries were still colonies, were born as citizens of the United Kingdom and Colonies. But when the countries became independent, people who had been born there became a citizen of that country (i.e. a St Lucian or a Jamaican citizen). If this happens to you, you could apply for a passport to the High Commission of the country which now claims you as a citizen. Or, if you've lived in the United Kingdom for five years, you could apply to be registered as a United Kingdom citizen and apply for a UK passport again. If you're under the age of 18, your parents would need to make the application for you.

11

Punishment

Parents have the legal right to decide how you should be punished. They are allowed to use corporal punishment — which usually just means a slap for a young child. But if your parents beat you hard, they can be prosecuted for assault. The court would then have to decide whether the punishment was 'moderate and reasonable', depending on how old and how strong you are. If your parents hit you excessively, you should get help from a friendly teacher or the local social services department.

If your parents separate, who will look after you?

If your parents separate or decide to get divorced, they may disagree about whether you should live with your father or your mother. If this happens, a court has to decide what parent you will live with. This will usually either be a magistrates' court, if your parents are separating but not getting divorced, or a divorce county court or the High Court if they are getting a divorce.

When a court decides who is to have custody of you, it must first decide what would be best for you. It should take your views into account, although this will depend on your age and how intelligent the court thinks you are. Usually, very young children stay with their mother. It is extremely rare for a father to get custody if he has never been married to the mother: this might only happen if your mother had neglected you, or was in prison or for some reason the court thought she was quite unsuitable to look after you.

If your parents are in dispute about who should have custody of you and any brothers or sisters you may have, you should get a visit from a social worker who will then report back to the court. You should see the social worker by yourself, and explain as clearly as you can what you think you would like best.

The Court can ask the Official Solicitor — who is a lawyer working for the court — to represent you where your parents disagree about custody. The Official Solicitor will get a report from the social worker who sees you.

It is very unlikely that you and your brothers or sisters will be split up. Usually, the court will decide to award both 'custody' and 'care and control' to one parent. 'Custody' means the right to take important decisions about your life, like what school you go to, what religion you belong to, what medical treatment you have and so on (as we explained earlier on page 8); 'care and control' means the day-to-day responsibility of looking after you. Occasionally the court may award 'custody' to both your parents, who should then consult each other about the decisions on important matters, while giving 'care and control' to the parent you will be living with.

Usually the court will say that the parent you are not living with should have 'access' to you i.e. the right to see you regularly. The court may say when and where this should happen (e.g. every other weekend) or it may leave things flexible.

Fostering

You may be looked after by 'foster parents' — people who aren't your natural parents, but who take you into their family. Your parents might, for instance, decide to have you fostered if they didn't want you adopted but couldn't look after you themselves — possibly because your mother is in hospital, or because they can't find a home for the family. Foster parents don't take over the legal rights and responsibilities of your natural parents, so that your parents still have to make the decisions about where you go to school and so on.

You may be placed with foster parents by the local authority after you have been taken into care. If this happens, then the local authority takes on the legal powers of your natural parents and the authority (i.e. the social workers looking after you) will make the decisions about your schooling, religion, medical treatment etc. The local authority is responsible for making sure that your foster parents look after you properly. More about care in chapter 3.

Foster parents can apply to adopt you if you have been with them for twelve months, but this is unlikely to be granted if your own parents have kept in touch with you. (See below for more on adoption.)

If you have lived with your foster parents for five years, you can only be taken away by your own parents if the court agrees.

Adoption

About 500,000 people in this country (including adults) were adopted as children. Some people don't discover that they are adopted until they reach their teens — and a few people may never be told. Other children are told that they are adopted as soon as they are old enough to understand.

Being adopted means that your new, adoptive parents take over all the legal rights and responsibilities of your parents: in law, your adopters become your parents. Once you have been adopted, any links with your natural parents will usually be ended completely.

In some cases, however, your mother and her new husband may have adopted you jointly: so that your adoptive mother is also your real mother.

The law recognises that many adoptive children want to know

who their real parents were, or may even want to go and see their natural father or mother. Once you reach the age of 18, you have the right to see your birth record which will tell you the name of one or both of your natural parents. You should apply to the Registrar of Births, Deaths and Marriages, 10 Kingsway, London WC2 (01-242 0262) or at the local registry office (in the phone book).

If you were adopted before 12 November 1975, you have to have an interview with a counsellor provided by the registrar's department before you will be shown your birth records. If you were adopted after that date, it is up to you whether you see the counsellor.

You can only be adopted on the order of a court, and your natural parents have the right to object. But the court can overrule their objections. When deciding whether or not to make an adoption order, the court has to give first consideration to the need to safeguard your well-being until you are an adult. If you were adopted when you were a baby or very young child, no-one will have asked you your opinion. But if you are adopted when you are older (and children can be adopted up to the age of 18), the court should find out what your wishes are and, as far as possible, take these into account.

Guardianship

Your parents and the courts have the power to appoint someone to be your guardian. Your parents may do this in their will to make sure

"I appoint my brother, Mr. V. Lusty, to be the guardian of such children of mine as are minors ....."

Your parents may appoint a guardian in their will to make sure there is someone to look after you if they die.

14

there is someone to look after you if they die. Normally, guardians are only appointed where your parents are dead or have deserted you. Your guardian will be the person who has custody of you, and usually has the power to administer your property, if you have any. Your guardian also has to consent to your marrying, if you are under 18. But your guardian must act in accordance with your best interests and can be removed or replaced by the courts.

Ward of court

Being made a ward of court usually only happens in an emergency — for instance, if your parents are separated or divorced, and your mother thinks your father will take you out of the country against her will and she has no other way of stopping him. (It could be the other way round, of course.) Or someone close to you (for instance, a teacher or welfare worker) can apply to have you made a ward of court if she or he thinks that your parents are making a decision which will be very bad for you (see page 11 for an example of this).

Local councils may also apply to have a child made a ward of court in order to keep you in care, although it is more usual for them to apply for a care order (as explained on page 37).

If you are made a ward of court, the court itself takes the place of your parents when it comes to making the main decisions about your life — what school you go to, where you live, what medical treatment you have, and so on. But you will go on living at home, unless the court decides that it would be better for you to be placed in the care of the local authority. If that happens, you would probably live in a community home or with foster parents (see page 35).

If you are a ward of court and want to marry before you reach 18, the court has to agree. This also applies if you want to leave the country.

Leaving home

Most people leave home because they have a job and are earning enough to live independently, or they are going away to study. But problems can arise, either if you want to leave home before you're 18 and your parents don't want you to, or if you leave home without enough money or anywhere to go.

If your parents don't object to your leaving home before the age of 18, and you keep out of trouble, you shouldn't have any difficulties. But if they do object and ask the police to find you, or if you come to the attention of the social services department or the police, you may find yourself in front of the courts — even though you haven't broken the law. This is more likely to happen to a girl since, if you are sleeping with someone you're not married to, the police

15

or social workers may decide you are in 'moral danger' and need 'care and control'.

If you are taken to court, your parents might have to promise the court to keep proper control over you, or the court may appoint a social worker to keep an eye on you. Or you may be placed in the care of the local authority (see chapter 3 for details).

You'll be less likely to end up in court if you have a job and can share accommodation with a friend of the same sex and generally give the appearance of leading a respectable life — and, of course, if you can avoid your parents complaining to the police. Things will be far more difficult if you are under 16, since you probably won't have a job or any income, and if you leave school to get a job you can be taken to court for not attending school.

Once you are 18, you can live where you like.

Many towns and cities have places where you can get advice — about where to live, the law and so on. There are some addresses on page 108, or you can ask the local Citizen's Advice Bureau.

2

SCHOOL

This chapter is an A to Z guide ('Attendance' to 'Uniform' anyway!) to how the law affects school-pupils and their parents. You can get more information from the books and organisations listed on page 3.

Attendance

Education is compulsory in this country from the age of five until 16. The local council (called the Local Education Authority or LEA) has to provide enough schools for the children in their area. Most children and young people go to schools run by the LEA, which are free, although some go to private schools where parents have to pay. If your parents don't send you to school at all, and the LEA think you are not getting a proper education, they can serve a notice on your parents requiring them to convince the LEA that you are being properly educated. If your parents satisfy the LEA, that will be the end of the matter.

If the LEA think that you should be going to school, they will tell your parents which school to send you to. If you still don't go, the LEA will probably send your parents a *school attendance order* naming the school you have to go to. Your parents can be taken to court if they don't obey the order, and if they are found guilty they can be fined up to £200.

See *Truanting* for what happens if you are sent to school, but don't turn up regularly, and *Leaving school* for when you can leave.

Changing things at school

If you have difficulty understanding a teacher or keeping up with the work, you should talk to your teacher about the difficulties. If a number of you are concerned about some aspect of the school – rules on uniform, for instance – you should get together to decide what to do. You might decide that you should all try and see the head-teacher, or if this doesn't work write a letter to the governors.

Your school may have a school council or some other democratic procedure which allows you to raise issues and have them discussed by pupils and teachers. If your school doesn't have one, you might talk to other students about pressing for a school council.

If your parents are worried about the education you are getting or the way the school is run, they should talk to the head-teacher. If they're still not happy, they could go to the school governors or managers (see under *Governors*) or to the local education authority (see under *LEA*).

You might also want to contact the National Union of School Students (NUSS) for advice, if you feel strongly about an issue and aren't getting anywhere.

Choosing a school

In some places, particularly in the country or a small town, there will only be one or two schools which you could go to. In a city, however, there may be a number of schools fairly near where you live. The LEA has to decide which school you will go to. They may consult your teachers (for instance, if you're moving from primary to secondary school). They must take your parents' wishes into account. But they don't have to ask you what you think.

If you feel strongly about which school you want to go to, or would like to find out more about the different schools available, you should tell your parents, who can go and visit the schools and see the head-teacher. Here are some questions which your parents could ask the head-teacher:

— How many pupils are there? (you or your parents may prefer a smaller school)
— What subjects are available? (for instance, what languages are provided?)
— Does the school timetable allow you to combine a variety of subjects, for instance science/languages/history?
— How does the school deal with 'girls" subjects and 'boys" subjects? Does everyone have to do both (for instance, domestic science and metal work)? Does the school encourage girls to choose only 'girls" subjects and boys to choose only 'boys" subjects?
— What are the school rules? (for instance, concerning uniform)
— What kind of punishment does the school use? Is there corporal punishment and, if so, how often is it used, who decides to use it and so on?
— Is there any rule forbidding pupils participating in political activities outside school hours?
— Does the school forbid you to join the National Union of School

Students?
- Is there a school council or any other way in which pupils can jointly raise issues with teachers?

Obviously, there are plenty of other questions to be asked, depending on your particular interests and preferences.

Once you and your parents have decided which school you most want to go to, they should notify the LEA. The LEA will try to send you to that school, but they don't have to if the school is full, or outside the area where you live, or if they think it is too far away or unsuitable for any other reason. You have the best chance of going to the school of your choice if you already have a brother or sister there, or if your parents have chosen it for religious reasons, or because they particularly want a single-sex or co-educational school, or because it provides special facilities which you need (e.g. if you are physically handicapped, or if you have a particular talent for which the school provides).

If you are refused a place at the school you have chosen your parents may be able to appeal to the LEA or sometimes the Secretary of State for Education.

Some parents who can afford it make sure their child gets into the school they want by moving into the area covered by the school. Others feel that the best thing to do is to get involved in the Parent-Teachers Association, become active in school affairs and try to make the school work the way they want. Occasionally, parents who feel very strongly about which school their child should go to refuse to send the child to school until they get their way. Sometimes they succeed; but they may be served with a school attendance order (see page 17) ordering them to follow the LEA's decision.

If your parents decide to send you to a private, fee-paying school, then the choice of school is up to them, provided, of course, that the school has a vacancy and you meet the entrance requirements.

Department of Education and Science (DES)

The DES is the government department which has the overall responsibility for making sure that schools are provided throughout England and Wales.

The DES is responsible to a Cabinet Minister, the Secretary of State for Education. In some cases, the Secretary of State can deal with an appeal by parents against the LEA's decision not to send their child to the school they want, or a decision to suspend or expel a child. The DES cannot control what subjects are taught in schools, or how they are taught. (Only religious instruction and physical education are compulsory). But they send inspectors to schools to make sure that the standard of work is satisfactory.

The DES is at Elizabeth House, York Road, London, SE1 (01-928 9222).

Discipline

The head-teacher is responsible for discipline in the school. So s/he can decide on the rules which you have to obey. The rules can say what you have to wear to school, whether or not you can smoke, whether any particular shops are out of bounds, what punishments can be imposed if you break the rules, and so on. In one court case, the court decided that it was perfectly all right for pupils to be ordered to run errands for the teachers.

The rules can also be used to forbid you getting involved in any political activity at school — for instance, joining the National Union of School Students or SKAN (School Kids Against the Nazis) or distributing their literature. Some schools have stopped pupils distributing National Front literature.

Head-teachers are also allowed to make rules about what you do outside school. They can forbid you to smoke, even if your parents don't mind. This kind of rule has also been upheld by the courts.

The head-teacher may consult the teachers and governors before making the rules. Some schools have councils, which give pupils a say in making the rules. But it is up to the head-teacher whether or not you are allowed to have a school council.

You and your parents can ask for a copy of the school rules. But you don't have any legal right to see them. Workers in a factory or office do have a legal right to see rules made by the employer, and there is a Government Code about these rules. Perhaps there should also be a Government Code on school rules?

Discrimination

It is unlawful for a school or an LEA to treat you unfairly because of your race or sex. Single-sex schools are still allowed, but the LEA must make sure that, overall, girls and boys get the same educational provision within that LEA's area.

Here are some examples of unlawful **sex discrimination**:
— Refusing to let girls do woodwork, or technical drawing or engineering because they are 'boys'' subjects.
— Refusing to let boys do cooking, sewing or home economics because they are 'girls'' subjects.
— Saying that you can only do technical drawing if you have previously done metalwork. (Since hardly any girls do metalwork, this rule in effect discriminates against girls by preventing most of them from doing technical drawing).

20

- Giving different punishments for boys and girls, such as caning for boys and detention for girls.
- Applying a quota to the numbers of each sex who can enter the school.
- Providing different facilities for boys and girls to do gym. But schools are allowed to discriminate when it comes to sport, by banning girls from, say, football and cricket.

Unlawful **race discrimination** includes applying a quota to the numbers of pupils from different racial groups who can come to the school. 'Bussing' children from one area to another in order to get a 'racial balance' in each school is also unlawful. Treating children of any particular race less favourably is unlawful.

If you think your school or LEA is discriminating, you or your parents should raise it with the teachers. The head may decide that the situation should be changed. You can get the Equal Opportunities Commission, the Commission for Racial Equality or NCCL to help (addresses on page 32). If this doesn't work, they can help you take the LEA or school to court.

For more information, see *Taking Liberties*, by Jean Coussins, or *Sex Discrimination in School*, by Harriet Harman (see page 31).

Expulsion

You should only be expelled if you do something very seriously wrong. If your parents think the decision to expel you was wrong, they can appeal to the Secretary of State for Education. (The Advisory Centre for Education can advise on this; address on page 32).

But if you are expelled from one school, and you are under 16, the LEA either has to find you another school or arrange for you to be educated in some other way, for instance by providing a home tutor. In practice, it may be some time before other arrangements are made.

Private schools (dealt with below) make their own rules about expulsion.

Free Schools

Free schools have been set up in a few places as an alternative to conventional education. They are private schools which don't charge a fee. Some parents choose to send their children there, because they object to the education provided in other schools.

An LEA may send a persistent truant to a free school in the hope that s/he will do better there. Free schools allow pupils more choice in what they do, and encourage children to make their own decisions and rules instead of having to obey someone else's rules. You can get more information about free schools from *Education Otherwise,* The Manor, Thelnetham, Diss, Norfolk.

Governors and managers

Every state school must have a board of managers (for infants and primary schools) or board of governors (for secondary schools). Some schools may be grouped together to share one lot of managers or governors.

Each board of governors or managers has a list of Articles which set out the different responsibilities of the LEA, the governors and the head-teacher.

In most schools, governors are involved in choosing (or sacking) the head-teacher, deputy heads and teachers; fixing holiday dates; deciding how the school spends its money; and deciding whether to suspend or expel a pupil.

Govenors are appointed by the LEA and usually include a number of people connected with local politics. Some schools have parent governors and teacher representatives. A few have pupil governors although there are legal difficulties in appointing a governor under 18 if the governors have financial responsibilities for the school. A recent committee on school governors recommended that all governors should include representatives of the parents and staff.

How much the governors get involved in the school depends very much on the interest they show and the extent to which the head-teacher tries to involve them.

You probably won't see much of your school governors, except on occasional visits or at assemblies or speech-days. But if you have an important complaint about the running of the school (for instance, sex or race discrimination) and the head-teacher hasn't convinced you there's a good reason for the situation or hasn't dealt with your complaint, you may want to bring it to the attention of the governors. If you can find out who the parents' representative on the board of governors is, ask him or her to raise it. Otherwise, ask the school or the local town hall for the name and address of the chairman of the governors and write to him or her.

Health service

All LEAs have a school health service which is now run by the National Health Service. It organises regular, compulsory medical inspections at school. If your parents don't let you go, they can be fined. They also provide dentists, and special clinics if you have special problems (such as bedwetting, or if you seem to be emotionally disturbed).

Homework

Most secondary schools and some junior schools set homework. There are arguments for and against homework, although obviously it's bad if you're set too much and can't do it in the time available. The law is very unclear about whether or not you can be forced to do it or punished if you don't. In one case, a court decided it was unlawful for a teacher to punish a pupil for failing to do his homework. But this probably only applies to junior schools. It seems likey that secondary school have a legal right to set homework and punish you if you don't do it.

Inspectors

Some inspectors are employed by the Department of Education and Science which is a national government department (see *DES*). Others work for the LEA. The inspectors make regular checks on schools and are mainly concerned with the standard of work being done in the school. They can advise teachers about teaching methods, subjects and curriculum. If they feel a school is being very badly run, they may report this to the DES or the LEA who can decide what action to take.

LEAs are responsible for providing adequate facilities for education and sport, although what is considered adequate varies from area to area.

Local Education Authority (LEA)

There are 104 LEAs in England and Wales who are responsible for providing educational facilities in their areas. In London, the Inner London Education Authority is responsible for providing facilities for all the inner London boroughs. Each LEA is run by the Chief Education Officer, who is responsible to the local council's Education Committee which consists of elected councillors.

The LEA has to provide enough schools for each area. They may also be responsible for organising special schools for backward or handicapped children or slow learners; transport to and from schools; providing playing fields; and running the careers service.

The LEA is not directly involved in the running of your school. This is done by the governors or managers, and the head-teacher.

Leaving school

Education is compulsory from the age of five until 16. But you can't actually leave school on your 16th birthday. A set of rules decides the date when you can actually leave. These are as follows:

1. If your birthday is between 1 September and 31 January, you can't leave school until the end of the spring term following your birthday.

2. If your birthday is between 31 January and the Friday before the last Monday in May, you can't leave school until that Friday (this is called the May school leaving date).

3. If your birthday is between the May school leaving date and before 1 September, you can also leave on the May school leaving date.

Meals

The LEA has to run a school meals service providing a mid-day meal for all the pupils at their schools. A charge is made (25p going up to 30p in autumn 1979) although families on low incomes can apply for free meals (see *Money*). The government decides how much should be charged, but an LEA can decide to spend more than that on each meal. School meals used to be free for all pupils, and ought to be made free again.

Milk

Free milk is provided for all children up to seven; pupils up to the age of 16 in special schools; and the handicapped children aged 5-16 who are not at school. Some schools provide free milk for all children up to 11.

In addition, children in families on low incomes can apply for free milk (see *Money*).

Money

Your parents may be able to get money from the local council for:
- your school uniform and other essential clothing;
- maintenance for you if you stay on after 16;
- transport to and from school (see also *Transport*, page 30);
- boarding school fees, if boarding is the only way you can get a a proper education.

They may also be able to claim free school milk or free meals for you.

Most LEAs have a scheme for giving School Uniform Grants to parents of secondary school children. Some LEAs use the same income figures as they use for free school meals for working out whether or not you qualify: these are set out below. Others are meaner, and use lower income limits. Some LEAs give cash, others give vouchers for use at shops selling uniform.

If your parents are on supplementary benefit, they should certainly be able to get a uniform grant. They should apply first to the local education council and then, if they're refused, apply to the social security office and tell them that the council have turned down the application. Sometimes the council and the social security office disagree about whose responsibility it is to pay for clothing and uniforms.

Some LEAs provide maintenance payments to parents on low incomes, whose child stays on at school after the age of 16. The ILEA, for instance, provides a weekly grant of £7.50. Sheffield has a similar scheme. But it is entirely up to the LEA whether or not to run such a scheme. The last Labour Government proposed to introduce a maintenance grant for pupils staying on at school after 16, but a pilot scheme in some parts of the country was abandoned when the Government fell in May 1979.

The head-teacher of your school may also be able to find money to pay for special provisions e.g. hire of a musical instrument.

If you or your parents want to find out more about education grants you should contact the LEA (look in the phone book under the name of your council, or ask at the town hall). It's a good idea to apply early in the year, before the LEA's money runs out.

If your parents are claiming supplementary benefit or family income supplement you will be entitled to **free school meals**. But you still have to fill in an application form, which you get at the education office, town hall or social security office.

Otherwise, free school meals go to children whose parents have incomes below a set level. For instance, a family with one child and an income of less than £40.15 a week qualifies. This figure is for the parents' income, *minus* tax and national insurance; rent, rates or mortgage payments; the first £4 of your mother's earnings (or the first £2 of your father's casual earnings if he is unemployed; or the first £6 of a single parent's earnings) and some other items.

The more children in a family, the higher the income limits. For instance, a family with three children could claim free school meals for all the children if the family income was below £53.35 after taking away all the items allowed. If the three-child family's income was between £53.35 and £55.85, then they could get free meals for one or two of the children but not all three.

All the figures were correct in November 1978, but they go up every year.

Because the rules and figures are so complicated, it's very hard to know if you're getting the free meals you're entitled to. You should contact the Child Poverty Action Group for help (address on page 32).

Private schools

Your parents can decide to have you educated privately, in a fee-paying school. Strangely enough, the posh private schools are called public schools.

You and your parents should look at the school prospectus and rules, and any other information you can get, to find out what the school views are on uniform, punishment and so on, and what kind of subjects and facilities they provide.

Your parents can complain to the Secretary of State for Education if they think the school premises are unsuitable, or if the proprietor or any teacher is unfit for the post.

Most children are educated in state schools. Most of this chapter does not apply to private schools.

Punishment

While you are at school, teachers have the power to punish you — provided the punishment is 'reasonable'.

Detentions should only be given for a good reason. They must be supervised by an adult and extra traffic hazards for children kept in late must be taken into account. Your parents can forbid the school to keep you in after school hours, but the school will usually then punish you in some other way.

Each LEA makes its own rules about corporal punishment — which includes any physical punishment such as hitting you on the hand with a ruler, or caning you. Schools are meant to keep a book

Because you're a damn nuisance, Jones, that's why!

A teacher has the powers to punish you as long as this is reasonable.

which records corporal punishments, although it often isn't kept properly. Your parents cannot insist on a teacher using corporal punishment on you. If they keep you away from school in order to stop you being caned, they may be prosecuted for not sending you to school. It is better for them to complain to the LEA and, if necessary, arrange a transfer to another school. If a teacher gives really heavy corporal punishment, causing physical harm, s/he can be prosecuted, and your parents should report him or her to the LEA and the police.

The National Union of School Students, NCCL and the Society of Teachers Opposed to Physical Punishment are campaigning to end corporal punishment (addresses on page 32). The United Kingdom is one of the few countries in Western Europe which allows school-pupils to be beaten. The Inner London Education Authority has banned corporal punishment in primary schools, and each LEA has the power to ban it in their schools.

Religion
Your school has to run a morning assembly so that all the pupils can join in what the law calls 'collective worship'. The school must also

run religious education lessons. The assembly doesn't have to be Church of England, or even Christian, and some schools try to run an assembly which people of many different religions can join in. The LEA can arrange for you to have different religious education from the course usually taught at your school: this can be done at your own school, or at a different school provided it doesn't interfere with your other lessons.

Your parents can withdraw you from religious instruction and morning prayers, by writing to the head-teacher. But you don't have any right yourself to withdraw from religious instruction or worship.

School attendance order see Attendance

School records and reports

Most schools send parents a regular report on their child's progress.

In addition, schools keep secret records about their pupils. Not all schools keep the same kind of reports and the quality and form they takes varies greatly from LEA to LEA. Some include your photograph as well as details about your academic progress and information about your behaviour, appearance, family and friends. Sometimes this information is recorded not in words but in points (e.g. you will be rated 0 to 10 for 'honesty', 'leadership' etc) to make it look more scientific.

There are no legal controls on the keeping of school records or who sees them. Neither you nor your parents have any legal right to see them, although they may be shown to a large number of other people – including a new school, an education welfare officer, social worker, probation officer or even the police. The records may also form the basis for a reference given by your school to a prospective employer or college. If you are taken to court, the LEA may have to provide a report on you to the court, and may do so by basing it on your school record.

School records are meant to give teachers full information about pupils so that they can do their job properly. But some records contain inaccurate, irrelevant or out-of-date information. NCCL and the Advisory Centre for Education (addresses on page 32) want to see these records opened to parents and pupils aged 16 or over.

Special education

The LEA can make special provision to meet the particular needs of some children, for instance:
– special schools for blind, deaf or handicapped children;

28

- special classes or schools for children with learning difficulties;
- home tuition for children who cannot get to school or who would find it embarrassing to attend. This could apply to a pregnant school-girl, or to someone who has been suspended and who doesn't have a place at another school.

Parents should be consulted about the decision to classify their child as 'educationally subnormal' and in need of special education. If they disagree with the decision, they can appeal against it, and can get advice from the Advisory Centre for Education (address on p.32).

Subjects

The head-teacher has the right to decide what subjects are taught at your school. S/he will usually consult with the LEA and the other teachers — but it is most unlikely that anyone will ask you for your views. The head-teacher also decides on the timetable, which of course can restrict the actual choice of subjects open to you.

If you want to do a subject which your school doesn't provide, you should ask the head-teacher whether arrangements could be made, for instance by sending you to another school for that subject. If two subjects you want to do (e.g. metalwork and home economics) are timetabled at the same time, you should also ask the teacher and the head to reconsider their decision. But if they don't change the timetable, all you can really do is get your parents to try and transfer you to a school which can meet your needs better.

Suspension

Suspension is increasingly used as a punishment. It means that you are temporarily banned from the school. Normally you should only be suspended for a serious reason. Only the head-teacher can usually make the decision, although in some areas the head can only suspend you if s/he gets the governors' consent. In some schools, you have the right to appeal to the governors against the decision to suspend you. You should ask a teacher, or insist that the head-teacher tell you or your parents what your rights are.

The school should tell you how long you are suspended for. Some don't, and this may be illegal. You should complain to the LEA if you are suspended indefinitely.

If you think the suspension was unreasonable, your parents can appeal to the Secretary of State for Education (see *Department of Education* above).

The LEA must make arrangements for you to be educated else-where while you are suspended, but there may be a long delay before another school or a home tutor is found for you.

Pupils have been suspended for wearing jewellery to school, not wearing proper uniform, or distributing NUSS or SKAN literature, as well as for serious misbehaviour such as hitting a teacher or another pupil, refusing to work or being absent for a long period without a good reason.

Transport

The LEA has to provide free transport to and from school if:
— you are under eight and the school is more than two miles away by the shortest possible route;
— you are eight or over and the school is more than three miles away.

The LEA can refuse to pay for your fare if there is a suitable school within that distance but your parents have chosen one further away.

The LEA can also, if it wants to, provide free travel for handicapped children or if they think it would be dangerous for you to walk home. If your parents have a low income, they can ask the LEA to pay your fares to school, even if you live within the two or three mile limit. If you think there is a special reason why you should get help with transport, it is always worthwhile getting your parents to ask the LEA.

Truanting

If you have never started at school, your parents can be compelled to send you there (see *Attendance*). Once you are enrolled at a school, your name is entered on the school register. The school has to inform the LEA if any of its registered pupils is not attending regularly or has been absent for more than two weeks without a medical certificate. It is not an excuse if you have to stay home because someone else in your family is ill.

The LEA will then send an **educational welfare officer** to see you and your parents to try and get you to go to school. If the police pick you up while you're truanting, they can take you into police custody and refer you to the educational welfare officer.

If you still don't go to school, the LEA can take your parents to court for 'failing to secure your attendance'. Your parents will have to convince the court that:
— you were absent with the school's permission; *or*
— you were unable to go to school because you were ill or because some unavoidable reason prevented you from going.

If you were sent to school not wearing the proper uniform, and your parents knew you would be sent home for that reason, they can be convicted for failing to make sure you went to school.

Your parents can be fined up to £200. If they are convicted three or more times for failing to get you to go to school, they could in theory be sent to prison, although this doesn't happen in practice.

Fining or imprisioning your parents isn't likely to be a very effective way of making you go to school. Some LEAs recognise that many pupils truant because they are bored at school, and have opened special truancy projects for young people who refuse to go to school. These projects have only a small number of pupils and aim to give students more relevant work then their school-courses may do. If you persistently truant, you might be taken into care by the local council (see chapter 3).

Uniform

The LEA, the school governors and the head-teacher between them decide whether or not your school has a uniform. If it does, you will have to wear it. Your parents can apply to the LEA for a grant to help with the cost of the uniform (see *Money*, page 25).

If you don't obey the school rules on uniform, the school can send you home. If this happens repeatedly, your parents can be taken to court for failing to make sure that you go to school (see *Truanting*).

Rules on uniform can forbid you to wear jewellery. In one case, a girl who wore earrings in her pierced ears was refused entry by the school, and her parents were convicted for failing to send her to school. Boys may also be refused permission to grow beards, and girls may be banned from wearing trousers.

If you object to your school's rules on uniform, you should talk to the teachers and the head. Your parents could also take the matter up with the Parent-Teachers Association, the board of governors and the local council's education committee.

More Information

You can get more information, or help and advice, from the books and organisations listed below.

The Parent's Schoolbook, Judith Stone and Felicity Taylor (Pelican, 90p). Useful for pupils too.

The Little Red Schoolbook, Soren and Jasper Jensen (Stage 1, 30p). The publishers were prosecuted when the first book came out, because of the way it talked about sex. It's not banned, but bits had to be cut out.

Sex Discrimination in Schools, Harriet Harman, NCCL, 75p.

Taking Liberties, teaching pack on sex discrimination and equal opportunities by Jean Coussins, Virago, £2.95.

Teachers and the Law, G.R. Barrell, Methuen, £6.95. Comprehensive guide to educational law; useful for parents and students as well as teachers.

Advisory Centre for Education (ACE), 18 Victoria Park Square, London, EC2 (01-980 4596). Can advise parents and pupils on education problems.

Commission for Racial Equality, 10-12 Allington Street, London SW1 (01-828 7022). Deals with complaints of race discrimination.

Child Poverty Action Group, 1 Macklin Street, Drury Lane, London WC2 (01-242 3225). Information and help on education grants and other benefits.

Department of Education and Science, Elizabeth House, York Road, London SE1 (01-928 9222).

Equal Opportunities Commission, Overseas House, Quay Street, Manchester (061-833 9244). Deals with complaints of sex discrimination.

National Council for Civil Liberties, 186 Kings Cross Road, London WC1 (01-278 4575). Deals with race and sex discrimination complaints. Campaigns against corporal punishment. Would like to hear from parents and pupils who've tried to open up school records. Does not deal with educational problems generally.

National Union of School Students, 302 Pentonville Road, London N1 (01-278 3291) (temporary address); 3 Endsleigh Street, London WC1 (01-387 1277). Organisation of school students; has produced a charter of school students' rights.

Society of Teachers Opposed to Physical Punishment (STOPP), 10 Lennox Gardens, Croydon, Surrey CR0 4HR.

3
CHILDREN AND YOUNG PEOPLE IN CARE

If you are 'in care', the local authority will appoint a social worker to look after you. S/he will decide where you live, what school you go to, where you spend your holidays, how often you see your family and so on.

You may be allowed to go on living at home even though you are in care, although if this happens the social worker is still responsible for supervising you. Alternatively, you may have to live in a community home, or you may be placed with foster parents.

When you are in care the local authority assumes responsibility for you.

About 100,000 children are in care in this country — and the numbers are growing. For every 1,000 people aged under 17, about seven are in care.

Why someone is put in care

Here are some examples of the things which may lead to your being taken into care:

— Your parents are dead or have abandoned you, and there is no relative to look after you properly.
— Your parents are ill or homeless and temporarily unable to look after you.
— You are being neglected or ill-treated at home, or in danger of this happening.
— You are under school-leaving age and persistently truanting and your parents can't or won't get you to go to school.
— You are in 'moral danger' (for girls under 16, this usually means sleeping around or being a prostitute; for boys, it usually means being at risk of homosexual contact. It also applies if you are sleeping rough, taking illegal drugs or thought to be mixing in 'bad company').
— You have been convicted of a criminal offence.

You won't necessarily be taken into care even if one or more of these things applies to you. We set out in detail below how children and young people can be taken into care (see pages 37-45).

A care order can be made on you until you reach the age of 18. Care orders usually end on your 18th birthday. But if you are taken into care at the age of 16 or 17, then the order sometimes lasts until you turn 19. No care order can be made on you if you are 16 or over and married.

Getting yourself put in care

Some people are so desperate to leave home and get away from their parents that they actually try to get the council to take them into care. In fact, you have no right to insist on being taken into care. You can ask the local council's social services department, but they can only take care proceedings if one of the things mentioned by the law applies to you (these are described briefly above, and are set out in detail on pages 40-41). They cannot take you into care simply because you feel your parents are behaving unreasonably by not letting you go out in the evenings or at weekends. But if you are being battered, or sexually assaulted, or otherwise very badly treated at home, then you should certainly go to the social services department for help.

Where you will live if you're in care

You can't choose where you will live once you've been taken into care. This is one of the most important decisions which the local authority will take for you. Usually they will want you to stay at home, or with foster parents, or in a community or voluntary home.

Each local authority has a register of approved **foster parents**, who are people willing to look after other people's children. The council has to approve foster parents before they can foster children in care. If the council fosters you with a family, the council will pay your foster parents an allowance for looking after you. The amount varies from authority to authority and usually goes up as you get older.

Community and voluntary homes

Community homes, which are usually paid for and run by local authorities, vary a great deal as they are designed to meet the needs of different children. Some are more secure, since they are designed to cope with children who would run away if they got the chance. Some have only younger children, others only have handicapped children, and so on.

There are government regulations on the way community homes are run and the facilities provided. The home must have adequate medical and dental facilities, and proper fire and safety precautions. The home must have facilities for family and friends to visit, although it is up to them to decide whether and when you can have visits. As far as practicable, the home must make arrangements for you to go to the religious services for your religion.

Young people who have reached the age of 16, but who are under 21, can go on living in a community home if they are working, training or studying nearby.

Voluntary homes, which are similar to community homes, are run and sometimes paid for by voluntary bodies, such as a charity or a church. Before a local council can send children to a voluntary home, they must inspect it to make sure it meets the required standards. The home then has to be regularly inspected to make sure it keeps up to scratch.

If you are living in a community or voluntary home, the local authority can insist that your parents pay something towards your upkeep. The amount they are asked to pay depends on their income, and in many cases parents are not asked to make any contribution. The amount involved cannot be more than the amount paid by the council to foster parents in its area. If the council and your parents can't agree on the sum they should pay, the council can ask the local magistrates' court to decide the amount.

The council can pay your parents' travelling expenses to visit you.

Your rights if you are in care

Young people don't have many rights under the present law, and this is even more true of young people in care. However, the local authority must act in your best interests and should, wherever possible, take account of your feelings before making decisions about you. They don't have to consult you if they think 'the interests of the public' demand otherwise (for instance, if you have been convicted of a serious crime). The council has to review your case every six months.

If you are in a home, the people running it and your social worker will decide the rules about staying out in the evening or at weekends, how much pocket-money you get and so on. They also make the rules about punishments. Corporal punishment is still used in community homes, although it has to be 'reasonable'. Being locked up in solitary confinement is also used as a punishment, although you should not be locked up for more than 48 hours.

Until you are 16 you cannot choose your own religion. Your parents can't insist that you are brought up in their religion, but they can stop you being brought up in a religion they disapprove of.

You can't be adopted while you are in care unless your parents agree, although it is possible for the court to do this without your parents' agreement if, for example, they think your parents are unreasonably refusing to agree. This could happen, for instance, if you have been with foster parents ever since you were very young and your natural parents have hardly kept in touch with you at all.

If you have to have medical treatment, the local authority has to consent on your behalf until you reach the age of 16. If you want to get married, they have to agree to this until you reach the age of 18. If you want to emigrate, they have to agree to this until you reach the age of 18.

You can apply to be taken out of care. A solicitor can act on your behalf and can be paid from the legal aid fund. On page 46, we suggest some ways to get legal advice.

Your parents' rights and duties

When you are in care, your parents will normally have to contribute money towards the cost of maintaining you. (See above, page 35.)

Your parents must tell the local authority their address, and any change of address, while you remain in care.

When a care order is made to take you into care, your parents must *not* keep you at home without the consent of the local authority. If they disobey the care order, they are committing a criminal offence and could be prosecuted.

Your parents cannot withhold their consent to your having medical treatment or an operation, or getting married, if you are in care. It is up to the local authority, not your parents to decide whether to agree. But your parents must be consulted if you want to emigrate.

Your parents can't force the local authority to bring you up in their own religion. But they can insist that you are not brought up in a religion which they disapprove of.

How you can be taken into care

In some cases, you may be taken into care 'voluntarily' — in other words, the council doesn't actually get an order placing you in care. Alternatively, the council decides to pass a 'parental rights resolution' or get a court order to take you into care. Or you may be taken into care because you have been convicted of a criminal offence. We explain firstly when you can be taken into care 'voluntarily'. The court orders which can put you in care are dealt with on pages 40-43.

Voluntary care

Voluntary care does *not* mean that you volunteer to go into care. But if, for instance, your parents are ill they can ask the local council to take you into care until they are well enough to look after you again.

You can be taken into care without any care order being made if:

— you have no parent or guardian;

— you have, but they have abandoned you;

— you are lost;

— your parents or guardian are unable to look after you (e.g. because they are in prison).

You can only be taken into voluntary care if you are under 17. You can then be kept in care until your 18th birthday. But the council will usually want to get you back to your parents as soon as possible.

Your parents can take you away at any time — although if you have been in voluntary care for over six months, your parents must give 28 days' notice to the council before taking you away. They can either write to the council saying they want you back, or they can just tell the social worker or the person running the home where you are living.

Keeping you in care

If you are in voluntary care, the council may decide that it would be better for you to stay in care rather than go home — for instance, if you're in danger of being battered if you return home. They can keep you in care by passing a **parental rights resolution** which is a formal decision by the council to take over the legal responsibility for looking after you. You will then stay in care until you are 18 (unless the council decides to end the parental rights resolution), and you will go on living where your social worker decides. Your parents would only be able to get you back if the council agreed, or if they went to court and got the court's permission.

The council may decide to pass a parental rights resolution about you if:

— your parents are dead;

— they have abandoned you;

— they are unable to look after you, for instance because they are ill;

— they are considered unfit to look after you, perhaps because the local council thinks their way of life is unsuitable (for instance, if your mother is a prostitute);

— the council thinks your parents have consistently failed to carry out the usual duties of a parent (e.g. they haven't fed and clothed you properly);

— the council has decided to take your brother or sister into care;

— you have been in voluntary care for three years.

Parental rights resolution

If a parental rights resolution is passed about you the main difference to you is that you can no longer go and live at home again unless the council lets you or a court agrees that your parents can have you back. You may not even know that the parental rights resolution is being passed until it's over. The next section describes the legal formalities which are involved in a parental rights resolution. Skip it if you're not interested in the legal stuff, but it may be useful if you're trying to get out of care.

If the social workers looking after you decide that the council should pass a parental rights resolution, they will probably hold a 'case conference' to discuss you, possibly inviting other people – for instance, a probation officer or education welfare officer – who have been involved with you. Neither you nor your parents are likely to be invited to the case conference, although you and your parents may be told it's happening.

The social workers then report to the council's social services committee who can recommend to the full council that they pass a parental rights resolution on you. Again, it is very unlikely that you or your parents will be invited to the council meeting.

The council may write to your parents, or send a social worker to see them, to find out if they will agree to the parental rights resolution. If they agree to this in writing, you will be kept in care.

If your parents don't agree in writing, the council has to serve them with a notice saying that the resolution has been passed and that they have the right to object. You have no right to object yourself, but if you don't want to stay in care, you should try and persuade your parents to object.

If your parents want to object to the parental rights resolution, they have to write to the council within one month, saying that they object. The parental rights resolution will then automatically end – unless the authority arrange for your case to be dealt with by the juvenile court. If they do this within 14 days of getting your parents' objections, then the resolution stays in force until the court has heard the case.

Most councils who have gone to the trouble of passing a parental rights resolution aren't going to let it drop just because your parents have objected. So what usually happens if your parents object is that the matter ends up being heard by the local juvenile court – and you stay in care until the court decides what should happen.

At the juvenile court, your parents have the right to be represented by a lawyer and can apply for legal aid to cover the costs. Although no-one is accusing you or your parents of committing a crime, the actual procedure in the court is very similar to that in a criminal case (which is described on page 94).

After they have heard all the evidence, the magistrates have to decide whether the local authority had good reasons for passing the parental rights resolution when they did; whether those reasons still exist; and whether it is in your interest for you to stay in care.

If the decision goes against them, your parents can appeal to the family division of the High Court. They will need a solicitor to organise this.

A parental rights resolution stays in force until you are 18. But your parents can apply to the court at any time to have it ended.

When the court orders you to be taken in to care

The local authority can go to court because they think you ought to be in care. Or a juvenile court can decide to put you in care because you have been convicted of a criminal offence. But you may, of course, be allowed to go on living at home even after a care order has been made.

There are two main kinds of court orders:

— care orders

— place of safety orders.

Care Proceedings

You may be taken into care if one or more of the following conditions applies to you and if the juvenile court thinks that you will not get proper 'care and control' unless you are taken into care. Usually, the local council will apply to take you into care, but the National Society for the Prevention of Cruelty to Children (NSPCC), the police or the local education authority can also apply in certain circumstances.

You could be taken into care if the court is satisfied that any of the following things applies to you:

— Your proper development is being unnecessarily prevented or neglected.

— You are being ill-treated.

— The court has decided that one of your brothers or sisters is being neglected or ill-treated and they think you are likely to suffer in the same way.

— One of your parents, or a step-parent, or someone else living with you or coming to live with you has been convicted of a crime involving cruelty to children.

— You are exposed to 'moral danger'. If you are a girl under 16 this means sleeping around or being a prostitute. Even if you are 16 or over, you can still be in 'moral danger' if you are sleeping around or mixing in what the court thinks is bad company. If you are a boy, 'moral danger' can mean being 'at risk' of homosexual contact. Taking illegal drugs, going to clubs late at night, living in a mixed flat or commune or sleeping rough could also lead the court decide that you are in 'moral danger'. But you are less likely to end up in court if you can give the appearance of leading a respectable life — sharing accommodation with someone of the same sex, for instance — and if you can avoid your parents complaining to the police or the social services department. Things will be a

And where do you think you've been?

A juvenile court can make a care order if it is satisfied that you are not under the control of your parent or guardian.

lot more difficult for you if you are under school leaving age, since you probably won't have any money, and if you leave school to get a job this could be a reason for taking you into care.

— You are beyond the control of your parent or guardian.

— You are guilty of a crime. But if you are found guilty of murder or manslaughter, you cannot be put in care: you would be sent to prison or borstal instead.

— You are not going to school regularly (this only applies if you are under school-leaving age).

If the court decides that one of these reasons applies to you, and that you are in need of 'care and control', one of the following things will happen:

1. Your parents may have to promise to take proper care of you and exercise proper control over you, for up to three years (or until you turn 18). If they don't do this, they can be made to forfeit up

to £200 to the court, and you could be taken into care by the council.

2. The court may pass a supervision order, appointing a social worker to keep an eye on you for a certain period. You will probably still live at home.

3. The court may make a full care order. The social services department of the council takes over responsibility for you, as explained earlier on page 35. If you are under 16 when the care order was passed, it can last until you turn 18. If you are older than that when it is passed, it can last until you are 19.

4. The court can decide to send you to mental hospital, or have a guardian appointed to take care of you. But this would only happen where they decided you were suffering from certain kinds of mental illness.

The next section explains the legal formalities in care proceedings: skip this if you're not interested in the legal details. On page 45, we explain what to do if you (or your parents) want to get you out of care.

Before the court hearing

If the council wants to take you into care, they normally start by informing the clerk of the local juvenile court what the grounds are for the care proceedings. The court should then send a copy of this notice to you, your parents and anyone with whom you have lived for more than six weeks in the last six months (usually your parents, but it could be your foster-parents, or a relative). If you are being taken into care because you have been accused of a criminal offence, and you are aged over 13, the local probation officer also has to be told.

After that, you and your parents should be sent a summons, telling you the time and the place where the case will be heard. In some cases, the council will want to take you away from your home before the case is heard: they can do that by applying for a place of safety order.

Place of safety orders

Probably the first thing you or your parents will know about a place of safety order is when the social worker (often with police officers) arrives at your home to take you away.

A local authority social worker (or the police, the NSPCC or anyone concerned with your welfare) can apply for a place of safety order if s/he thinks you are being ill-treated or neglected, or in danger for any other reason. (This includes 'moral danger', as explained on page 40). Usually neither you nor your parents is told that this is happening, and the local magistrate will make a place of safety order without hearing what you or your parents have to say. The magistrate should listen to the evidence of the social worker or official making the application, and should only make the order if s/he is satisfied that you are genuinely at risk. Orders are rarely refused.

Once a place of safety order has been made, you will be moved to a community home, a foster home or in some cases a hospital. It is an offence for your parents to refuse to obey the place of safety order. You have no right to appeal against the place of safety order, and nor have your parents. It will last for up to 28 days, by which time the local authority should have started care proceedings.

So once a place of safety order has been made, you just have to wait for it to run out. But you should use the time before the court meets to get yourself a lawyer, as explained in the next section.

Getting a lawyer

In care proceedings, the court has to consider *your* interests and should decide what is best for you. Your parents, of course, should also be present in court and have some rights to express their views.

You can be represented at the court by a lawyer, who can be paid for out of legal aid. You (or your parents, your social worker or a friend) can get the legal aid forms from the court. Your parents can represent you themselves – but this may not be a good idea if you and your parents have any disagreement. They can also instruct a lawyer and get legal aid on your behalf but neither they nor the lawyer should forget that the lawyer is acting for *you*, not your parents. Your parents cannot get legal aid for themselves except where an application is being made to end the care order and the local authority doesn't object.

You can find a lawyer by asking the local Citizen's Advice Bureau for the names of lawyers doing legal aid work. If there is a local law centre (in the phone book or ask the CAB) you should ask them whether they can represent you. You should then talk to the lawyer, and make sure that s/he explains what is going on so that you understand it fully. You should tell the lawyer how you feel about what is going on: whether you think that being taken into care is the best alternative, or whether you would prefer to stay with your family.

Temporary care orders

When the case comes to court, you may find that the court is not ready to deal with it — perhaps because the social workers haven't had time to talk to you and your parents and prepare a report. If this happens, the court can put off the case (it's called an adjournment) and make a temporary care order, putting you in the care of the local council until the case can be hear. The temporary order is called an interim care order, and cannot last for more than 28 days. They can go on making new interim care orders until the case is heard — so that you could be taken into care temporarily for months on end.

You or your lawyer can object to an interim care order being made. If it is made anyway, you can appeal to the Crown Court. You can also apply to the High Court to have the order overturned or ask the Juvenile Court to discharge the order. Your lawyer should explain these possibilities, and take the necessary steps.

If you are taken into care under a temporary order, you may still be allowed to live at home. But if the council thinks it is urgent to get you away from your home (for instance, if they believe you are at risk of being battered), they may insist that you go and live in a community home.

At the court

On the day when the case is due to be heard, you and your parents and your lawyer will have to turn up at the court. This will be the local juvenile court and the people who will deal with your case are local magistrates. You should usually be there unless, of course, you are ill, although the court can order that a child under five doesn't have to come. If the court thinks that you may be upset by hearing all the evidence, or that this would be unsuitable for you to listen to, they will probably talk to you at the beginning of the case and then ask you to leave.

At the beginning of the case, the magistrates should explain to you or your parents why the care order has been applied for and what the case is about. After that, people speak and witnesses are called in much the same order as in a criminal case — even though care proceedings are *not* criminal cases. (In chapter 9, we set out in detail the order in which things happen in a criminal case.)

If the council wants to take you into care because they say your parents aren't looking after you properly, your parents should be given a chance to question the council's representatives or any witnesses the council calls. Your parents can also call their own witnesses, or speak to the court themselves, to explain why they think they are looking after you properly.

If, after listening to all the evidence, the magistrates decide that the local council is right, they can also look at written reports prepared by social workers, probation officers or education welfare officers. On page 95, we explain what rights you and your parents have to see these reports.

At the end of all this, the court decides whether to get your parents to promise to look after you properly, or whether to make a supervision order or a care order. These were explained on page 42.

Other ways the court can order you to be taken into care

In addition to the legal procedures outlined above, the local council can apply to have you made a ward of court. (See page 15 for more on this).

If your parents are getting divorced and there is disagreement about who should have custody of you, the court may also decide that it would be better for a care order to be made. This could also happen in a case about whether or not you should be adopted. Finally, the court could order the local council to take you into care if you are convicted of a criminal offence. (See chapter 9 for more on criminal proceedings.)

Getting out of care

Once a care order has been made, it stays in force until you are 18. (If you were 16 or 17 when it was made, it stays in force until you are 19).

If you wish, you can appeal against the care order immediately after it is made. You have to do this within 21 days and the appeal goes to the Crown Court (which has a judge who is more senior than the magistrates who heard the first case). You should talk to a lawyer about an appeal immediately after the care order is made.

Once you have been taken into care, you or your parents can apply at any time to the juvenile court to have the care order ended. If you fail the first time, you have to wait at least three months before applying again. Again, you should contact a local law centre or get a lawyer to help you if you want to have your care order ended.

If you or your parents apply to have the care order ended, and the local council doesn't try to stop you, the court can appoint someone to act for you. This person is called a guardian *ad litem* and is likely to be a social worker. The guardian can appoint a lawyer to represent you and should also talk to you and your parents and anyone who has been looking after you. The guardian has to produce a report for the court.

If a guardian is appointed to represent you, then your parents are also entitled to get legal aid and have a lawyer to represent them.

If your parents have applied to take you out of care, and you don't want to go back to them, you should tell the social worker and any lawyer involved exactly how you feel about it. You should, of course, have plenty of opportunity to talk to the social worker and the lawyer without your parents being present.

If the court decides to end the court care order, they may substitute a supervision order — which means that you live at home under your parents' care, but a social worker is appointed to keep an eye on you and them. Or they may simply end the care order without putting anything in its place.

It is often difficult for people who leave care at the age of 18 to find a place of their own to live. Social workers can help you buy the things you need (e.g. cooking things for your bedsitter or flat), by getting money from the local council.

Further information

Guide to Care Proceedings, Family Rights Group (75p including post), 24 Romilly Road, London N4.

Voice of the Child in Care, c/o 60 Carysfort Road, London N8 (01-348 2588). A support group for children and young people in care.

4 EMPLOYMENT, UNEMPLOYMENT JOB TRAINING

The law on what age you can do various jobs is complicated, and its effect varies from area to area. Broadly speaking, the rules are as follows:

If you are under 13, it is illegal for you to work unless you have an entertainment licence (this is explained below).

If you are aged 13, 14 or 15, you can take a part-time job, for not more than two hours on any school day. You can't work during school hours (9am to 4.30pm including the lunch hour). You can't start work before 7am or go on after 7pm.

"Dear Teacher, I hope you enjoyed the champagne......"

The dinner break is part of the school day and you cannot use it to work in.

On Saturdays, you can work for eight hours, but only for two hours on Sundays.

But your local authority can make regulations which apply locally and which may be stricter than these general rules. You can get a copy from the town hall.

The local authority can stop you doing any job at all if it thinks that the work will interfere with your education or welfare. If it thinks the job will damage your health or education, it can serve a notice on your employer forbidding him to employ you or imposing conditions on your employment.

You can only do 'light work', so you are not meant to do work involving heavy lifting. You cannot engage in street trading.

Under the age of 17, you are banned from working in manufacturing, demolition, mining, building or transport industries. Most local authorities have local rules banning you from working in kitchens, cake shops, restaurants, slaughterhouses, billiard saloons, gaming or betting shops or any business requiring door-to-door selling or touting.

No-one under 18 is allowed to be employed in a bar.

These rules are very frequently broken. Someone who employs you in breach of the law can be prosecuted and, if he is convicted, fined. But this happens very rarely.

If you are aged 16 or over and have left school, you are free to work under the same conditions as adults. (There are, however, laws limiting the hours young people can work). But if you stay on at school after 16, the Local Education Authority (LEA) can impose conditions on you remaining at school — for instance, making it a rule that you don't have a part-time job.

Markets and street trading

In general, you are not allowed to work on a market stall or become a street trader until you are 17. But some local authorities let you work on your parents' stall once you reach the age of 14. Ask at the town hall for details. Again, this rule is often broken and rarely enforced.

Entertainment

You cannot usually have time off school to take part in plays, films, TV shows or other entertainments unless you have a licence from the local authority. You will only get a licence if the LEA is satisfied about the arrangements made for your education and welfare. The licence will specify the times you can be absent from school.

You can get more information on this from a book called *The law on performances by children* published by Her Majesty's Stationery Office (write to HMSO, High Holborn, London WC1).

You don't need a licence to perform in things like the school play or the occasional charity performance.

Earnings

Any money you earn is legally yours, not your parents. Although you can be taxed, the number of hours you can work is so restricted you are unlikely to earn enough for this to happen. The wages paid to school-children are notoriously low, and many employers will use you as cheap labour.

Conditions at work

The conditions under which people work are controlled by law. All offices, shops and factories must have a certain number of toilets; premises must be kept clean; there must be proper fire precautions; and the building must be safe. There should be a notice on display setting out the regulations.

At the age of 16, you can join a trade union. Unions provide valuable benefits for their members, particularly by negotiating better wages and conditions. If you are sacked or victimised, your union should fight the case. If you are injured at work, the union can advise you on getting compensation, and many unions pay sick pay for their members. Find out who the shop steward or union representative is at your place of work. If you're not sure which union to join, contact the Trades Union Congress, Great Russell Street, London WC1, who will tell you.

When you start work for more than 16 hours a week, you should get a statement of the terms and conditions of employment, telling you what your pay is, whether you will get sick pay or holiday pay, and so on. If you don't get this statement, ask for it.

Detailed information about workers' rights and the law is contained in *Your Rights at Work* (published by NCCL, 70p).

The Armed Forces

A boy can join the armed forces at the age of 16. Girls can join at the age of 17. But you need your parents' agreement until you are 18.

If you join before you are 17½ (boys) or 18 (girls), you can leave within the first 6 months by giving 14 days' notice. You don't have to pay anything to leave.

Boys who join between 17½ and 18 can leave within the first six months, or before they reach the age of 18 and 3 months. They have to pay £20.

After that, it gets much more difficult to leave the armed forces.

That's what I think of punch operating!

The Careers Officer will be able to advise you on the different jobs available.

Getting a job

The careers teacher at your school or college should discuss with you the various kinds of work available and help you decide what to do. S/he should also know about the different training schemes.

You should make up your own mind about what work you want to do, and while most careers teachers will try to find a job that suits you, a few will try and make up your mind for you. This is particularly true for girls who are often pushed into so-called 'women's' jobs such as clerical or shop work. But sex discrimination is now unlawful and if you want to do a job that is traditionally thought of as 'men's work' (or if you are a boy and you want to do an untraditional job such as secretarial work), you should not let yourself be pressured into something else.

The careers teacher should be able to help arrange interviews with prospective employers.

If there is no careers teacher or adviser at your school or college, you should contact the careers officer for your area (look in the phone book under the local education authority).

Job Centres

As well as looking in local papers for jobs, you can visit the local Job Centre (look in the phone book). Job Centres, which are run by the government, have a large number of jobs displayed on cards. You just pick the card which interests you, take it to the receptionist who will fix an interview for you. But a Job Centre cannot give you detailed advice or help about which job is suitable for you.

Youth Opportunity Programmes — if you're unemployed

If you are aged between 16 and 19 and don't have a job, you should be eligible for a place on one of the special schemes run by the government for young people. The careers officer or local job centre can tell you about the schemes. Here is a list of the different type of courses available:

— Employment Induction Course. This is to help you decide what kind of work you do and lasts about two weeks.

— Short Training Courses. These give you training for a specific job and last three months.

— Work experience with an employer. This gives first-hand experience of different kinds of work.

— Project-based work. This involves working on projects (e.g. clearing up and re-developing a local area) which gives you first-hand experience of different kinds of work. Lasts six months.

— Training workshop courses. Gives first-hand experience of work in a group producing goods or services. Lasts up to one year.

— Community Service. Gives first-hand experience of different kinds of work in local community activities.

— Occupational Selection Course. Prelude to a short training course; prepares you for work in a particular occupation.

The number of places available on these courses, and the type of schemes involved, may change as a result of the new Government's policies. You can get up-to-date information from the Job Centre.

Apprenticeships and day-release

Many employers offer apprenticeships or time off during work to allow you to attend college. The careers officer should be able to give you information about these. Now that the Sex Discrimination Act is in force, apprenticeships must be open to both boys and girls. Although far fewer girls than boys get apprenticeships, and most girls' apprenticeships are in hairdressing, there is nothing to stop you going for an apprenticeship for much better-paid work — for instance, as a printer, engineer or builder.

Some employers provide good on-the-job training, such as the civil service and local government. But you should ask any employer where you go for an interview what training opportunities they provide.

The *Personnel and Training Year Book,* published by Kogan Page, lists industrial training courses. Get this at the local library. You can also get an Index of Industrial Scholarships and Training Schemes from the Advisory Centre for Education (address on page 55).

Going to college

Many jobs require you to have GCEs or CSEs or other exams before they will employ you. If you didn't do them at school, you can do them later. Colleges of further education provide full and part-time courses, and you may actually prefer studying for the exams in a college where you are treated as an adult, rather than at school. The careers office can tell you about the courses available locally.

Further Education Colleges also provide a wide range of vocational courses (that is, courses qualifying you for a particular kind of job) on a full or part-time basis. Again, the careers office can give you information.

Studying for a degree

You can apply for a place at university or polytechnic when you are 17, although you can't actually enrol until you are 18. You should ask your teachers about the different courses available. You could also look at the *Directory of Degree Courses,* which should be at your local library. Another useful publication is *How to apply for admission to a university* (50p from UCCA, PO Box 28, Cheltenham, Gloucester GL20 1HX).

The Higher Education Advisory Centre, 114 Chase Side, Southgate, London N14 (01-886 6599) provides information on higher education courses and grants.

Grants

The LEA for your area must give you a grant to do a :

— first degree course;

— course recognised as equivalent to a degree course;

— Higher National Diploma Course;

— teacher training course;

— course leading to a diploma in Higher Education.

You may be refused a grant if you haven't been resident in the United Kingdom for the three years leading up to 1 September in the year when your course starts. But you will still get the grant if your parents or husband or wife were employed outside the UK during that time.

You may also be refused a grant if the LEA thinks your behaviour makes you 'unfit' to get a grant, or if you have already attended a course for which you got a grant, or if you are under 25 and have already attended two years' full-time further education outside the UK.

The amount of grant depends on the resources of your parents or your husband or wife. The National Union of Students (address on page 55) negotiates the level of grant with the Department of Education. The grant is meant to cover your fees and living expenses.

In addition, the LEA can award a grant for a course other than those listed above, or may give a grant to a student who wouldn't normally qualify. It is always worth trying. The NUS can advise you on the attitude of your particular LEA, and can advise on charities and trusts which may be able to help if your LEA won't.

Social Security benefits

If you are unemployed, you may be able to claim unemployment benefit. But you need to have paid national insurance contributions in work before you can get unemployment benefit, and it is therefore difficult for anyone under 18 to get unemployment benefit.

If you are over 16 and not in full-time employment, you can claim supplementary benefit. To do this, you must register as unemployed with your nearest Job Centre or Employment Exchange. If you are still at school, however, you won't normally get benefit since your parents should be maintaining you.

If you are doing a full-time course at university or college, you can't apply for supplementary benefit during term time, although you can apply during the vacation.

Supplementary benefit is worked out on a basic weekly 'scale rate' which goes up each November. In addition to that, you will normally get a sum to cover your rent. But if you are living at home, you would only get the 'non-householder' rate, which is lower, to cover personal expenses. If you are getting board and lodgings, you should get a sum to cover what you pay your landlord, plus a sum for personal expenses.

Your grant is supposed to include a sum equal to the 'non-householder' rate during the short vacations. So you would normally only be able to get a rent payment on top. The grant does not cover the long summer vacation, so you could claim full supplementary benefit then.

Where a married couple are living together, only the man can claim benefit for both of you. If the social security office decides you are 'living together as man and wife' then they will usually disqualify the woman from benefit, and insist that the man claims for both of them — which, of course, he won't be able to do if he is earning.

The supplementary benefits officer should give you a Notice of Assessment explaining how your level of benefit has been worked out. If you're not happy with it, ask him to explain or contact one of the organisations listed at the end of this chapter. They can help you with an appeal if you're not getting the right amount.

Students can also claim unemployment benefit during vacation, if they have paid or been credited with enough contributions to qualify.

Both CPAG and NUS (see page 55) can give detailed advice on claiming benefits.

Maternity benefits

If you're going to have a baby, you may be able to claim a maternity grant of £25. But either you or your husband has to have paid national insurance contributions at work. Unless one of you was in employment at least 16 months before the baby was due, and paid stamps for at least 25 weeks (six months), you won't qualify for maternity grant. Mothers under 16 can't get the grant.

Maternity allowance, which lasts for several weeks before and after your baby is born, depends on the contributions paid by the mother.

The rules about contributions, and the exclusion of mothers under 16 from benefit, means that the youngest mothers, who need the money just as much as other mothers if not more, can't get it. If you are having a baby and you're not married, you should claim supplementary benefits for the period when you don't work. If you are married and living with your husband, you can't claim supplementary benefit: only the man can claim and, of course, if he is earning he won't get benefit.

More Information

You can get more information from the following books:

National Welfare Benefits Handbook (CPAG, 70p) and *Students' Rights Guide* (CPAG, 70p) both by Ruth Lister.

Your Rights at Work, by Patricia Hewitt (NCCL, 70p).

Welfare Manual, published by the NUS (£2.50), covers grants as well as benefits.

The following organisations may also be able to help.

Advisory Centre for Education, 18 Victoria Park Square, London E2 (01-980 4596)

Careers Research and Advisory Centre, Bateman Street, Cambridge (0223-6911)

Claimants Unions These are organisations set up locally by people claiming social security and supplementary benefits. The local law centre or CAB may know if there's one in your area; otherwise, ask other people at the social security office.

Child Poverty Action Group, 1 Macklin Street, Drury Lane, London WC2 (01-242 3225). Doesn't just help 'children'. Can advise on social security problems. Publishes extremely useful guides to welfare benefits.

Educational Grants Advisory Service, 26 Bedford Square, London WC1

Higher Education Advisory Centre, 114 Chase Side, London N14 (01-886 6599)

National Union of Students, 302 Pentonville Road, London N1 (01-278 3291)

National Advisory Centre on Careers for Women, 251 Brompton Road, London SW3 (01-589 9237)

National Institute of Adult Education, 35 Queen Anne Street, London W1 (01-637 4241)

TOPS, Training Opportunities Scheme, 162-8 Regent Street, London W1 (01-214 6000) or local 'skillcentres' or employment offices: training and retraining, with allowances, for people over 19.

Trades Union Congress, Congress House, Great Russell Street, London WC1 (01-636 4030).

University Central Council on Admissions, PO Box 28, Cheltenham, Gloucestershire.

5

MONEY AND PROPERTY

You are entitled to own money regardless of your age and if your parents are given money for you then they must normally hold it for you on your behalf. Anyone of any age can open a bank account, either a deposit account (where you earn interest on the money you keep in the bank) or a current account (where you have a cheque book but where most banks do not give you any interest). You may find, however, that banks are reluctant to let people who have not yet left school, and who therefore have no earnings, have a current account. This is because if you 'overdraw' (write cheques for more money than you have in the account) they cannot get it back from you as you have no earnings they can sue you for.

Special rules apply to the National Savings Bank. You cannot deposit money with the National Savings Bank if you are under seven years old unless someone over that age does if for you. You can deposit money in a Trustees Savings Bank at any age but if you are under seven you cannot withdraw it. If you are under seven and have money in either the National Savings Bank or a Trustee Savings Bank and it is proved to the bank that money is urgently needed for your maintenance, education or benefit or there are other reasons, then the bank can pay sums from the account to anyone who satisfies them that s/he will use the money for your benefit. Apart from these restrictions you can draw your money out as and when you wish.

Pocket money

There is no law that says that your parents or guardian have to give you pocket money.

Income tax

If you earn money then you have to pay income tax if your total earnings are more than the minimum level at which tax has to be paid. This figure is changed annually. In July 1979, the maximum you can earn in any week before paying tax is about £21. However if you earn more than this but you're not working full-time over a whole year then you may still not have to pay income tax, as it is the amount of money that you earn in the whole year that counts. In most jobs, the tax is deducted from your wages before you get paid. This is called PAYE, which stands for Pay As You Earn. So if you haven't worked for a whole year and you think you are paying too much tax speak to your employer and ask him/her for the address of the tax office.

Until you are aged 18 your father (or your mother if she has custody of you) should make a tax return for you on his or her income tax form. If your earnings have been taxed on the PAYE system then this is not a problem but if you have not been taxed then s/he will have to pay. Then s/he is entitled to keep money out of your earnings to pay this tax.

Of course many small employers who employ young people pay them out of petty cash or till receipts so that they don't have to account for the money. Then no one knows that you have earned the money and so you don't get taxed on it. This is not legal but the Inland Revenue doesn't seem to worry too much.

Contracts

In law, a contract is an agreement between at least two people. This means that just buying an article from someone means that you have actually entered into a contract with them. So obviously you enter into contracts well before you reach the age of 18.

Although you can enter into contracts before you are 18, the law treats you differently from adults in that in general you are not bound by the agreement even though the other party to it is. There are three main exceptions to this. The first arises where the contract is for the purchase of goods or services which are essential for you such as food, clothing, medicine, or somewhere to live. The law calls such goods 'necessaries'. The other two sorts of binding contracts are contracts for apprenticeships and contracts of employment.

In these three cases you are legally bound by the contract and can be sued if you break it. In other cases if you have acted fraudulently in breaking the contract you may be bound by it in law.

None of this stops you being a partner in a firm or a member of a company, building society or industrial provident society. If you are a partner in a firm, however, unlike adults, you are not liable for the firm's debts or the acts of your partners. Partnership assets can be used to pay off partnership debts before you get your share.

Liability for other acts committed by you.

You can be liable in law for certain types of behaviour if harm has resulted to others. Examples of this are trespassing on other people's property and causing damage, damage done by your pets, taking other people's property and selling it, damaging or refusing to return it.

You can only be liable for such acts if you are of such an age as to be able to distinguish between right and wrong. In certain circumstances your parents can be liable, for instance where they could have stopped you or if they allowed you to do the damage.

Borrowing money

There is nothing in law to stop you borrowing money at any age, but since in most cases the person who lends it to you will not be able to sue you for it if you can't repay it, you might well find it difficult to find someone prepared to lend it to you.

Property

While you are under eighteen years old you cannot own land or what the law calls real property. This includes houses, buildings of whatever kind and land regardless of what it is used for. This only applies to property in this country and different rules may apply to property situated abroad. If you inherit or otherwise acquire real property whilst you are under eighteen then it will be looked after by other people, known as trustees, for you until you are eighteen. Usually if you inherit property it will be under someone's will and this will provide the names or details of the trustees to look after it for you. If there is no will then the law still says that the property must be held on trust and a court can if necessary appoint trustees to look after it for you. Trustees have a duty to act in your interests and to manage the property properly. If they don't they can be penalised by the court.

6 SEX, RELATIONSHIPS AND MARRIAGE

This chapter is about how the *law* treats sexual relationships and marriage. We haven't tried to give detailed factual information about sex, nor do we discuss morality or the personal problems which arise in relationships. On page 69, we suggest some books and a number of organisations which can give you more help and advice.

The criminal law is much harsher on a boy who has a sexual relationship with a young girl than it is on the girl. This is because the law is based on the traditional idea of protecting helpless females from dangerous men. Furthermore, a boy is almost never taken into care on the grounds that he is in 'moral danger', unless he is thought to be having a homosexual relationship. A girl can be taken into care because she sleeps with her boyfriend, or is thought to be 'promiscuous'.

But the law is much tougher in theory than in practice. In 1977, only 42 boys aged under 17 and 559 men aged 17 or over were prosecuted for having sex with a girl aged under 16. Even the police say that this is a small proportion of all the cases known to the police (3,924 in 1977). And the cases known to the police are only part of the real total. The risk of prosecution is higher if the girl's parents complain to the police.

Homosexual boys and men are more likely to be prosecuted. In 1976, 86 boys under the age of 17 were prosecuted for homosexual relationships, and 216 men aged between 17 and 21 were prosecuted. Out of nearly 5,000 offences known to the police, only 2,750 adults and young people were prosecuted. So prosecutions only affect a minority of those involved in homosexual relationships.

Sex between males and females

It is illegal for a boy or man to have sexual intercouse with a girl who is under 16. This age is known as the age of consent. But a girl cannot be prosecuted for unlawful sexual intercourse if she has sex with boys of any age. She *could,* however, be prosecuted for indecent assault if the boy is under 16.

The age of consent was raised to 16 in 1885 to protect white young girls from prostitution and the 'white slave trade'. The law does not, of course, prevent many girls from deciding to have sex before that age — while, on the other hand many girls wait until they are older than 16 before having a sexual relationship. Defenders of the present law argue that it is necessary to protect girls from having sex before they are physically and emotionally ready.

It is illegal for a boy or man to have sexual intercourse with a girl who is under 16 although there is no such restriction on girls over 16 having intercourse with boys.

Girls

You cannot be prosecuted for having sex at any age. (The only exception is incest, which is explained on page 68).

Usually, the law will not interfere if you and your boyfriend decide to have a sexual relationship before you are 16. But if your parents object, or if you have left home, it is possible that the local authority might decide to take you into care on the grounds that you are in 'moral danger'. This can happen if the social workers think you are sleeping with your boyfriend or likely to, or if they think you are promiscuous or at risk of becoming involved in prostitution. You can be taken into care on 'moral danger' grounds even after you have reached the age of 16, when it is legal for your boyfriend to have sex with you.

Chapter 3 gives more information on being taken into care.

For advice on contraception, see page 64. We also list, on page 69, other books you can read about sexual relationships and places you can go to for help and advice.

Boys

If you are under 14, you cannot be prosecuted for having sex with a girl who is under age. Also you can't be prosecuted for rape (although you could be charged with indecent assault or attempted rape if you attack a girl or woman. More about the law on assault and rape on page 67).

If you are aged 14 or over, and have sex with your girlfriend before she reaches 16, you can be charged with 'unlawful sexual intercourse'. You could be fined, sent to borstal, attendance centre or detention centre if you are convicted. If the girl was aged 13 or over, and you haven't been charged with the same offence before, you can defend yourself if you had reason to believe that the girl was actually aged 16 or over. In practice, there are very few prosecutions of boys under 17.

If you are aged 17 or over, you could be sent to prison for up to two years if you are convicted of unlawful sexual intercourse with an under-age girl. (The prison sentence could be longer if the girl was aged under 13.) Provided you are under 24 and the girl was aged at least 13, you can defend yourself if you had reason to believe that the girl was actually 16 or over — provided, too, that you haven't been charged with this offence before.

If you and your girlfriend decide to live together, and she is under 16, you could be charged with taking an unmarried girl away from her parents. This can happen even if you don't have sex. If you are aged 17 or over, and are convicted of this offence, you could be sent to prison for up to two years. But prosecutions for this offence are hardly ever brought.

In theory, you could also be prosecuted if you take an unmarried girl *under the age of 18* away from her parents in order to have 'unlawful sexual intercourse' with her. 'Unlawful sexual intercourse' means sex outside marriage. (But don't worry: sex outside marriage is *not* a criminal offence). Your only defence is to show the court that you reasonably thought the girl was aged 18 or over. So, if your 17-year old girl friend leaves home to live with you, you could be prosecuted, even though she is over the age of consent. Fortunately, prosecutions are almost never brought for this offence.

Homosexuality

Homosexuality means sexual relationships between people of the same sex. Homosexual women are usually called lesbians.

A very large number of women and men who would not think of themselves as gay have had some kind of homosexual experience at some time in their lives. Some girls and boys experiment with their own sex before they get involved with someone of the opposite sex. Many young people have strong sexual feelings for people of their own sex; some of them will later form sexual relationships with people of the opposite sex while others will remain homosexual. Roughly 10% of the adult population is homosexual.

There is considerable ignorance and prejudice about homosexual relationships. Lesbians suffer from prejudice and discrimination, even though the law does not usually interfere with them. The law on male homosexual relationships is complicated and confusing, and treats all homosexual acts involving someone under 21 as illegal — even if both of you have agreed, and have enjoyed it.

It is not illegal for a woman to have a homosexual relationship with another woman, unless one of you is under 16 (or you are both in the armed forces when it is meant to be a threat to discipline).

Boys and men in homosexual relationships

It is illegal for you to have a sexual relationship with another boy or man until you are *both* 21. Even then, homosexual behaviour is only legal if it is between only two individuals, if both of you are aged 21 or over and consent, and it takes place in private.

Any homosexual relationship which doesn't fit that definition can be punished by the law. Someone involved in a homosexual relationship could be charged with any of the following offences:

— Buggery. This means anal intercouse, however slight. You can be charged with this if either of you is under 21, or if the act is not in private, or if one partner does not consent.

— Gross indecency. This covers any homosexual act between men, other than buggery. It is most often used where the police say the act was not in private (e.g. in a public lavatory, even behind closed doors) or if one or both of you is aged under 21. It includes mutual masturbation, or one of you masturbating the other. In 1976, 14 boys aged under 17 were prosecuted for indecency.

— Indecent assault. A man can be charged with indecent assault if his partner is under 16 (a boy aged under 16 is assumed incapable of consent), or if his partner is aged 16 or over but did not consent. 'Indecent assault' can include a wide range of acts, from just touching to buggery. It is not an indecent assault to invite someone to touch you.

— Importuning. If you repeatedly try to pick up another boy or man in a public place, you can be charged with 'persistently importuning for an immoral purpose' — in other words, soliciting. In practice, the police usually only arrest people for this in public lavatories or places well-known for pick-ups.

When you can be charged with a homosexual offence

Whether or not you or your partner is prosecuted for homosexual behaviour depends on how old you each are, the circumstances in which the act took place, whether you both consented and so on.

If you are under 14, the law presumes that you are incapable of sexual intercourse! So you can't be prosecuted for buggery.

If you are under 16, the law assumes that you are incapable of consenting to a homosexual relationship. (Just as it assumes that girls under 16 are incapable of consenting to a heterosexual relationship). Your partner, if he is older, could be prosecuted for indecently assaulting you, even if, in fact, you consented. If you touch or have sex with someone who is also under 16, or someone older who doesn't consent, then you could be prosecuted yourself for indecent assault.

If you are under 17, you could be taken into care on the grounds that you are in 'moral danger' because of your homosexual relationship. Or you could be placed under a supervision order, so that a social worker keeps an eye on you while you go on living at home. Obviously this won't happen if the local council's social workers don't find out about it, or don't think it is serious enough to justify taking you into care. (See chapter 3 for more on care and supervision orders).

If you are aged 16 or over, both you and your partner can be prosecuted for gross indecency or buggery. (The Director of Public Prosecutions has to give his consent to a prosecution involving a homosexual man under 21. So this does not often occur.)

Below we set out the *maximum* punishments which someone aged 17 or over could get for a homosexual offence if their case is heard in a Crown Court. The penalties in magistrates courts are much less severe. The penalties for someone aged under 17 are set out on pages 96-101.

— Gross indecency: two years' prison and/or a fine if you are both under 21; five years' prison and/or a fine if one of you is under 21 and the other 21 or over. The most common sentence is a fine.

— Indecent assault: 10 years' imprisonment and/or a fine.

— Importuning: two years' imprisonment and/or a fine.

— Buggery: life imprisonment and/or a fine if your partner is under 16. If you are both aged between 16 and 21 and both consented, the maximum is two years prison and/or a fine. If your partner was aged 16 or over but did not consent, the maximum is 10 years' prison and/or a fine. And a man aged 21 or over who commits buggery with a consenting man aged between 16 and 21 can get up to 5 years' prison and/or a fine.

At the end of this chapter, on pages 69-70, we list a number of organisations which give advice and support to homosexuals.

Contraception: girls

The age of consent doesn't stop some girls under 16 sleeping with their boyfriends. But it may be difficult for you to get advice on sex and contraception because of your age. If you are thinking of sleeping with your boyfriend, you must get advice on contraception — and don't let yourself be put off if your own doctor is unhelpful, or if you think he or she would tell your parents and you don't want him to.

If you are under 16, it is quite legal for you to use birth control. You can go to your family doctor or a family planning clinic for advice. Doctors are encouraged by the Department of Health to give under-age girls contraceptive advice and supplies without telling your parents, if you want to keep it confidential. Although it is technically illegal for a doctor to give you a medical examination or treatment (eg fitting the cap) without your parents' consent, the Department has told doctors that they are not breaking the law if they give you contraceptive treatment to protect you against an un-wanted pregnancy, even if they don't ask your parents' consent.

In the end it is up to the doctor whether or not he tells your parents. Some will refuse to help. Others will help and tell your parents. Others will help and respect your wishes about whether your parents are told or not. If you are worried about going to your own doctor, it is vital that you get advice from someone else, so you should go to a family planning clinic which will not tell your parents if you don't want them to. (The Brook Centre (see page 69 for address) specialises in helping younger girls.)

If you are aged 16 or over, whether you are single or married, you can get birth control advice and supplies from your doctor or local family planning clinic.

Contraceptives from a clinic or on prescription are free.

The most common forms of contraception for women are the pill, the IUD (intra-uterine device or coil) and the cap. At the end of this chapter we suggest some books and organisations which can give you more information.

Contraception: boys

Most forms of contraception so far developed are for use by girls. The exception is the condom (Durex) which can be easily bought at most chemists and barbers and is not expensive. Don't take the risk of making your girlfriend pregnant: either make sure she is using contraception, or use it yourself. Men can be sterilised (the operation is called a vasectomy), but this would not normally be done on a boy or young man.

Pregnancy

If you think you're pregnant, find out quickly. If you decide you do not want to carry on with the pregnancy, you will need to arrange an abortion as soon as possible. If you do decide to keep the child, then the sooner you start planning the better.

If you are under 16, you may not want your parents to know you are pregnant. You can go to your family doctor for a pregnancy test but — as with contraception — it is his decision whether or not to tell your parents. If you don't want to go to your family doctor, you should go to a local family planning clinic (see pages 69-70).

Many chemists advertise pregnancy testing kits which you can use at home. A positive result means you're pregnant. A negative result means you may be pregnant, and you should go to a doctor or clinic to check. If you find out you are pregnant, and don't want to talk to your parents you should go to your doctor, a family planning clinic, a sympathetic teacher or social worker, or someone else who can give you help and support.

If you are aged 16 or over, you should go to your doctor or family planning clinic to find out whether or not you are pregnant. They will treat your visit as confidential and cannot tell your parents without your permission.

Having a baby when you're under 18

Apart from the ordinary problems which may occur when you're pregnant, a number of particular difficulties can crop up if you are under 18.

If you're still at school, you may be reluctant to keep attending. You should ask the Local Education Authority if they will provide you with a home tutor during this time. If you're under 16, the LEA has to make arrangements for your education.

Sometimes parents react to their children's pregnancies very badly, and if this happens you should be able to get help and support from your local social services department who will usually take you and your baby into care if your parents refuse to let you stay at home.

If you're not married, you have legal custody of your child. Although parents and social workers may try to persuade you to let the baby be adopted or placed in care, the decision is yours. If you're worried or want advice, you should consult the National Council for One Parent Families, 255 Kentish Town Road, London NW5 (01-267 1361).

Mothers under 16 get no financial help from the state. The Labour Party has promised that maternity grant should, in future, be payable to all mothers regardless of whether they (or their husbands) have paid social security contributions. But mothers under 16 need the full range of financial benefits just like anyone else — as do other young mothers who may not have worked and paid contributions long enough to qualify for the full maternity allowance. If you are living at home, your parents may be able to claim supplementary benefit for you.

Abortion

If you are considering ending your pregnancy, you should try and talk it over with someone you know and trust, and discuss it with your own doctor or a counsellor at one of the pregnancy advisory services mentioned on pages 69-70.

If you decide on an abortion, you should have it as soon as possible. The later an abortion, the less safe it is. Menstrual extraction (which is a method of gently sucking out the contents of the womb after your period is late or within a few days of sex) has now been declared legal as a form of abortion. It is done even before you know you're pregnant, when the foetus, if there is one, is hardly developed at all.

An abortion needs the consent of two doctors. If your own doctor is unsympathetic, you should immediately contact one of the abortion advice agencies mentioned on pages 69-70. About half of all abortions are done on the National Health, although married women are more likely than single women to get an NHS abortion. The rest of abortions are done privately, many of them through non-profit-making charities. A private abortion in a non-profit-making clinic will cost about £65 – £80, although the price may be reduced if you can't afford it. If you are under 16, you need your parents' consent to an abortion. But the clinic may not check up on your age.

Living together

If you are aged under 18, you can live together as long as your parents or legal guardian don't object. If they do, they can stop you living together by having you made a ward of court (see page 15) or complaining to the police or the local council which might end up with the girl being taken into care.

Once you reach the age of 18, you can live where you want to, and with the person or people you choose.

The legal and practical disadvantages and advantages of living together or getting married are set out in *Women's Rights: A Practical Guide* (see page 69 for booklist).

Marriage

Getting married when you're very young may not be a good idea – particularly if you're getting married in order to get away from your parents, or because you're pregnant, or because you think mother-hood and marriage would be a better alternative to a boring job. Teenage marriages have a very high divorce rate, and single parent-hood, when you weren't preparing for it, can be very difficult indeed.

If you marry when you are under 16, then the marriage will be void – in other words not recognised by law.

If you are 16 or 17 and want to marry, you need the written permission of your parents or legal guardian (or the local council if you are in care) if you are being married in a registry office. For a church wedding, you don't need their consent, but the banns have to be read for three consecutive Sundays without any objection. In Scotland you don't need any permission once you're 16.

If your parents or guardian refuse to consent to your marriage, you can apply to the local County Court for permission to marry. You should see a solicitor about this, or go to the clerk's office at the local court (look in the phone book) for information. If you try to get married without your parents' or guardian's consent, they could apply to have you made a ward of court – in which case, you will need the permission of the court to marry. If you do manage to get married without their consent, then, provided you're aged over 16, the marriage will be legally valid.

Rape

A man or boy aged 14 or over, who has sex with a girl who does not consent — and the man knows that she didn't consent, or doesn't care whether she consents or not — has committed rape.

If you submit to sexual intercourse because you have been threatened or given drink or drugs, then you have not legally given your consent, and the man can be found guilty of rape.

A boy under 14 cannot be prosecuted for rape, although he can be prosecuted for attempted rape or assault. The maximum adult penalty for rape is life imprisonment. The sentences for boys under 17 are set out on pages 96-101.

The legal definition of rape only covers sexual intercourse (i.e. penetration by the penis into the vagina, however slight). Other forms of sexual assault are not, in law, rape: the man could be charged with indecent assault (maximum adult penalty two years' imprisonment) or with causing grievous bodily harm, or a similar offence.

Rape is particularly horrible and embarrassing for the victim. If you have been raped or sexually assaulted, whether recently or years ago, you can contact the Rape Crisis Centre on 01-340 6145 (24-hour phone) or 01-340 6913 (office hours) and they can provide advice, help and support.

Incest

Incest means sexual intercouse between close relatives — for instance, father and daughter, mother and son, brother and sister. Sex between half-sister and brother (i.e. two people with the same mother but different fathers, or vica versa) is also incest. Sex between cousins is *not* incest. Homosexual incest does not exist in law. Although very few people are prosecuted for incest (mainly fathers accused of having sex with their daughters), it is rather more common than generally realised.

If your father or another relative is forcing sexual attentions on you, you don't have to put up with it. But complaining could be very upsetting for you, since it means that the rest of your family will find out. You can go to an organisation like the Albany Trust, who should be able to help without bringing in the police. It may be possible for you to be taken into care for a while to get you away from the incestuous relationship. Alternatively, threatening to go to the police may stop the problem.

The same applies if you are being molested by any other adult, or in the smaller number of cases where a boy is receiving unwelcome attentions from a woman relative or another adult.

If you consent to an incestuous relationship (for instance, with your brother or sister), you can both be prosecuted. This happens very occasionally to adults who live together incestuously.

Further information

Many books on sex are uninformative or written in a very patronising way. You may find these useful:

Make It Happy, by Jane Cousins; a sensible book on sex education, written in ordinary language and full of practical help (Virago, £2.95)

Our Bodies, Our Selves, edited by Angela Phillips and Jill Rakusen; a book on health and sexuality for women, originally published in the USA but revised for this country (Penguin, £3.50)

Women's Rights: A Practical Guide by Anna Coote and Tess Gill; full of facts and background information, including a useful chapter on sex and the law (Penguin, £1.25)

Learning to Live with Sex; good short pamphlet (Family Planning Association)

Homosexuality and the Law; NCCL factsheet 5p plus 7p post

The Single Woman's Guide to Pregnancy and Parenthood, by Patricia Ashdown-Sharp (Penguin, 95p)

Pregnancy Month by Month and *New Born Baby* (Consumer's Association; £2.50 each)

The Sexual Behaviour of Young People (Penguin, 80p) by Michael Schofield; a study of sexual behaviour and attitudes.

Helpful organisations

Albany Trust, 16-20 Strutton Ground, London SW1 (01-222 0701); advice and counselling on sexual problems.

British Pregnancy Advisory Service, Guildhall Buildings, Navigation St, Birmingham 2 (021-643 1461) and 58 Petty France, London SW1 (01-222 0985); run a number of advisory clinics and nursing homes.

Brook Advisory Centres, 233 Tottenham Court Road, London W1 (01-580 2991), specialises in helping younger girls and has centres in Coventrey, Bristol, Birmingham, Cambridge, Liverpool and Edinburgh (addresses in local phone books). Completely confidential. You can phone, write or drop in.

Campaign for Homosexual Equality. PO Box 427, 69 Corporation Street, Manchester M60 2EZ (061-228 1985), information about gay, transvestite and transexual groups.

Family Planning Information Service, 27 Mortimer Street, London W1 (01-636 7866)

Family planning clinics – local clinics should be in the phone book under 'F'.

Friend, 274 Upper Street, London N1 (01-359 7371), information and support for homosexual and bisexual men and women. 7.30pm – 10pm every day

Gay Switchboard, c/o 5 Caledonian Road London N1 (mailing address only) (01-837 7324); 24-hour telephone advice service for gay people.

Gay Teenagers, 6-9 Manor Gardens, London N7 (01-267 5975; temporary number).

Grapevine, 296 Holloway Road, London N7 (01-607 0935/0949) free sex education advice and information service for young people Can put you in touch with organisations in your area.

Icebreakers, BM/Gay Lib London WC1 (01-270 9590); counselling and advice for anyone with a sexual identity problem.

National Council for One-Parent Families, 255 Kentish Town Road, London NW5 (01-267 1361)

Pregnancy Advisory Service, 40 Margaret Street, London W1 (01-409 0281), another non-profit-making organisation which gives counselling and arranges abortions.

Release, 1 Elgin Avenue, London W9 (01-289 1123; 01-603 8654 emergencies); can give advice on legal problems, abortions etc.

Sappho, 20 Dorset Square, London NW1 (01-724 3636), organisation of lesbians.

7

ALCOHOL AND OTHER DRUGS

The word 'drugs' covers a wide range of substances. Some are legal, some are not. The most common everyday drugs are tannin, found in tea, and caffeine, found in coffee. Nicotine, in cigarettes, is highly addictive and dangerous, and alcohol can also be a killer, if taken in large enough quantities. The laws on drugs are inconsistent and confused.

You'll kill me if you go on like this!

The word 'drugs' covers a wide range of substances. Some are legal, some are not.

Alcohol

It is often said that young people under 16 cannot drink alcohol legally. This isn't true. The law says that it is an offence to give alcohol to a child under five. Between five and 16, you are allowed to drink alcohol provided that you do so on private premises.

It is against the law for anyone aged under 18 to buy alcohol from pubs, off-licences or shops. Both you and the person selling you the alcohol can be fined up to £200. It is also against the law for anyone under 14 (apart from the landlord's own child) to go into a pub or licensed premises used for selling and consuming alcohol. Once you reach 14, you can go into a pub but you can't buy or drink alcohol there. Once you reach the age of 16, you are allowed to have beer, wine, cider or perry with a meal in a hotel or restaurant. At the age of 18, you are entitled to buy drinks in a pub and drink there.

Cigarettes

It is not illegal to smoke in private at any age. But it is an offence to sell tobacco, cigarettes or cigarette papers to someone aged under 16 when it is for that person's own use. You can also be taken to court if you are aged between ten and 16 and try to buy tobacco for your own use.

If you are under 16 and you are found smoking in a public place, a uniformed police officer or a park-keeper can seize all tobacco and cigarette papers (but not a pipe or tobacco pouch!)

Teachers may tell you that it is illegal to smoke before you are 16. It isn't — although the school rules may forbid it.

Illegal drugs

It is illegal to use, possess or supply certain drugs. These are divided into three classes. We give below the maximum *adult* penalty which applies for offences involving each class: see pages 96-101 for sentences which apply to young people.

Class A

These are the drugs considered to be most dangerous. An adult convicted of possessing any of them can be sent to prison for up to seven years. The police only have to prove that you were in possession of the drugs; it doesn't matter whether you had actually used them or intended to. The main Class A drugs are: heroin, opium, LSD (acid), injectable amphetamines and 'angel dust'.

Class B

These drugs aren't considered quite as dangerous as Class A but sentences are still high (five years' imprisonment and/or an unlimited fine is the maximum for an adult convicted of possession). The main Class B drugs are most amphetamines and amphetamine-related drugs, purple hearts, cannabis (both marijuana and hash), benzedrine and dexedrine.

Class C

This is the least serious group, although the maximum penalty which can be imposed on an adult for possessing a Class C drug is still two years and/or an unlimited fine. The main Class C drugs are Mandrax and similar stimulant drugs.

The Advisory Council on the Misuse of Drugs Act has recommended that cannabis become a Class C drug, and Mandrax a Class B drug.

There are many other substances which people take in some way to try and get 'high'. These are things like glue, aerosols or even fire extinguishers, all of which can be inhaled. In general these are all highly dangerous substances and can cause very severe damage to your body, especially your liver. Some of the chemicals in these substances are also carcinogenic (i.e. they cause cancer).

Selling illegal drugs

The penalties for selling illegal drugs are much higher than for possessing them. An adult found guilty of selling Class A or B drugs can be sent to prison for up to 14 years and also be heavily fined. Selling Class C drugs can get an adult up to five years in prison and/or a heavy fine.

Other offences

It is an offence to grow – or try to grow – a cannabis plant. It is an offence to allow your home to be used for people to smoke cannabis or opium, prepare opium or produce or supply any other illegal drug. It is a very serious offence to try and import illegal drugs into this country. And, if you are going abroad, the penalties for possessing or supplying cannabis or other drugs can be far more severe than in this country – and it is very difficult to get out of a foreign jail!

Police powers

The police can stop and search you in the street if they have 'reasonable grounds' to suspect you have an illegal drug. They can also stop and search your car. They are not meant to stop you just because you have long hair or dress differently or are black, but in practice they often do.

If the police have reason to believe you have committed an offence under the Misuse of Drugs Act, they can ask for your name and address. If you don't give it; or if they think you have given a false name and address; and if they think you will not turn up at court, then they can arrest you without a warrant.

Normally you will be released on bail by the police for up to three weeks while any drug they've found on you is analysed. You will have to report back to the police station on a specified date and, if the analysis is positive, you will be formally charged.

The police can also search your home to look for illegal drugs if they have a magistrates' court warrant.

Information and advice

Release, 1 Elgin Avenue, London W9 (021-289 1123; 01-603 8654 emergencies), can provide information, refer you to a lawyer etc.

Institute for the Study of Drug Dependence, Kingsbury House, 3 Blackburn Road, London NW6 (01-328 5541)

THE POLICE

You may come into contact with the police for all kinds of reasons. You may go to the police yourself if you've been attacked or robbed. You may ask them the way somewhere. They may think you've committed a crime and want to question you about it. They may want you to be a witness in a case against someone else. Or the police may decide you are at risk — perhaps because you're not being looked after properly at home — and decide to take you into custody for your own protection.

Most of this chapter is about what happens if you are suspected of committing a criminal offence. On page 85 we suggest what your parents or friends can do to help if you're arrested. On page 87, we discuss what happens to the victims of crime, particularly people who have been sexually assaulted or raped. And on page 86 we mention points to watch for if you are being questioned as a witness.

The age of criminal responsibility in England and Wales is ten. Below that age, you cannot be charged with a criminal offence, although you can be arrested and cautioned and you could be held under a 'place of safety' order if the police think you are beyond your parents' control or at risk of being injured. (More on place of safety orders on page 42). Anyone aged ten or over can be charged with a criminal offence, although it is rare for someone under 12 to be prosecuted. About two-thirds of 10 to 13-year-olds picked up by the police, and one-third of those aged 14 to 16 are cautioned instead of being prosecuted. More about cautions on page 80.

In the streets

If the police stop you, they won't necessarily tell you why. It may be because they're investigating a crime such as the murder of a child in the neighbourhood, and need as much information as possible from other young people. The police depend on getting the co-operation of possible witnesses, or people who knew the victim, when they are investigating crimes.

But if you think the police suspect you of doing something wrong, it is best to say as little as possible. Anything you say can be used as evidence in court — and it is very difficult to disprove their version of what you said. It is usually sensible to answer simple questions like 'What is your name and address?', 'Where are you going?' or 'Where have you been?' But if they go on questioning you, ask them what it is about and what they suspect you of. If they won't tell you or you're worried about what may happen, just say firmly that you don't want to answer any more questions. However upset or angry you feel, it's a good idea always to behave politely and respectfully to the police.

If you are stopped it is best to behave politely to the police.

The general rule is that *you do not have to answer any police questions.* If you are driving a car or you are suspected of having been involved in a car accident, you have to give them your name and address. Otherwise, if you refuse to give your name and address (or if they think you've given a false name and address), you can be arrested provided they think you've committed one of the following offences:

— a motoring offence (includes dangerous or careless driving of a

car, motor-bike or bicycle or driving without a licence or under age)
- possessing an illegal drug and they think you'll run off;
- possessing an offensive weapon in a public place;
- possessing a firearm illegally;
- not paying your rail fare or producing your ticket;
- stealing birds' eggs or breaking regulations in a Royal Park.

Police powers to stop you

The police do not have any general right to stop people in the street. But they *are* entitled to stop you if you are under 17 and they believe you are being ill-treated or neglected, exposed to moral danger or beyond your parents' control. This would apply, for instance, if you are found sleeping rough, staying out late, going to 'unsuitable' places and so on. The police can take you to the police station and may refuse to let you go home if they think you are at risk. (See page 83 for more on this point.) But they must tell your parents or guardians why they are keeping you.

In addition you can be stopped and arrested for 'sus' — being a suspected person loitering with intent to commit an arrestable. offence. This is explained in more detail in the section on arrest; see page 78.

The police can also stop and ask to **search** you if:
- they are looking for stolen goods (this applies in London, Manchester, Liverpool, Newcastle and most other major towns);
- you are suspected of destroying eggs of protected birds;
- they want to find out if you have any papers or articles on you which could provide evidence that you are involved in anything relating to terrorism.

The police must have reasonable grounds for suspecting that you have what they are looking for. Your clothes, the length of your hair, being black and so on are *not* meant to give the police 'reasonable' suspicion for drugs searches — although in practice the police often stop people for these reasons.

You can be charged with obstructing a policeman in the execution of his duty if you refuse to be searched or try to resist. Apart from the situations listed above, the police have no *general* power to search you, and can only do so if you agree. The problem is that if you refuse to be searched when the policeman thinks that it would be reasonable for an innocent person to agree, that may make him decide he has 'reasonable' grounds for arresting you.

What to do if the police want to search you

Before you agree to be searched:

1. Ask if you are being arrested.

2. Ask what the police are looking for and under what authority they intend to search you.

3. If they give no reasonable grounds for searching you, you need not agree to be searched.

4. In theory, you can use reasonable force to protect yourself against an unauthorised search. But if you get into a fight with the police, you may get hurt and you will probably be charged with assaulting or obstructing the police. It is better to say firmly that you have not agreed to be searched, and then take legal advice and make a complaint later.

5. If possible, make sure that anyone who is with you stays to watch you being searched. You may need them as witnesses.

6. If you agree to be searched but want it done in private, ask to be searched at the police station. Try and take witnesses with you. Remember that you are going voluntarily and can leave once you have been searched — unless you are then arrested.

At school

The police should *not* arrest you or come and question you at school. If this is essential, they should ask the head-teacher's permission and they should only interview you with the head-teacher or another adult present. If you are arrested or questioned at school unnecessarily, you should make a complaint (see page 85).

Arrest

If the police think you're committing an offence, or if they are not satisfied with the answers to their questions, they may decide to arrest you and take you to the police station. They may say 'We're arresting you', but they may not even mention the word 'arrest' but say something like 'You'd better come down to the police station'.

You should ask at this stage whether or not they're arresting you. If they are not arresting you, you do not have to stay. But running away is not a good idea, since it may provoke the police into arresting you.

If you are under 17, the police can detain you at the police station if they think you are being ill-treated or neglected, exposed to moral danger or beyond your parents' control.

Otherwise, the police should only arrest you for one of the following offences:

- Arrestable offences. These include theft, most offences of violence unlawful possession of drugs, taking and driving away a motor vehicle.
- 'Sus'. The police can arrest you if they believe you are a 'suspected person loitering with intent to commit an arrestable offence.' This gives the police a very wide power to arrest you on the streets, even if there is no evidence that you have committed an arrestable offence. It is especially used in London and Liverpool.
- Breach of the peace. This can be used if the police think that what you are doing will lead to a public disturbance.
- Obstruction of the highway. This allows the police to arrest you if, for instance, you are distributing leaflets and refuse to move on when they ask you. It is widely used at demonstrations and pickets.
- Having an offensive weapon in a public place. This has been interpreted in different circumstances to mean anything from a penny to a gun.
- Having an article used for theft.
- Refusing or failing to take or pass a breathlyser test.
- If you are a woman, you can be arrested if they suspect you are a prostitute soliciting in a public place.

The police should make it clear that they are compelling you to go with them. They should also tell you why they are arresting you unless this is obvious, or it is impossible (e.g. you run away or start to struggle). Ask why you are being arrested, and try to remember so that you can tell your lawyer later on.

Arrest with a warrant

In addition to the situations just listed, the police can also arrest people if they have a warrant for them. A warrant is a piece of paper granted by a magistrate, giving the police the power to arrest someone. If you are being arrested under a warrant you should check to see that you are the person named on the warrant. You should also check to see whether it says you should be released on bail. More about bail on page 83.

Police powers on arrest

Not all arrests take place on the street. The police can enter property, if necessary by force in order to arrest someone. If you refuse to let them in, they can prosecute you for obstructing the police.

Once you have been arrested, the police are allowed to search you. They can also search the place where you were arrested. They may also try to go to your home — if, for instance, you were arrested in the street — to search there as well, and it is difficult to stop this.

The police should *caution* you as soon as they arrest you, by telling you that you do not have to say anything unless you want, but anything you do say may be taken down and used in evidence. Remember that even though the police are not formally questioning you on the way to the police station, everything you say on the journey will be noted down and can be used in court.

At the police station

Even if you haven't been searched before, you will be searched when you arrive at the police station. Everything in your possession — keys, money, cigarettes, matches, jewellery, your watch and so on — will be taken away by the police and put in a polythene bag. You can only be searched by a police officer of the same sex as you. You should be asked to sign the list of things they take: sign immediately below the last item so they can't add anything.

You may be kept waiting a long time before questioning starts. You can be questioned in the detention room at the police station, or in the cells. The usual rules apply to answering questions in the police station: you don't have to say anything, and anything you do say can be used in evidence against you or another person.

The police may also ask you to make a statement and you don't have to.

The police may ask you to make a statement. You don't have to, and if you do it can be used in evidence.

Most people are very frightened when they are at the police staion. You won't know how long you'll be there for, whether you have to stay overnight, whether your friends or family have been told, or what's going to happen to you. It is very easy to say something you don't really mean. But once you have said something to the police, it's virtually impossible to withdraw it later. That's why it's usually better to say nothing until you've talked to a lawyer.

It is very easy to say something you don't mean at the police station. Below are two examples which illustrate this — each turned into a nightmare for the young people involved.

Mohammed, who was 17, worked as a petrol pump attendant at a garage in West London. His employer accused him of taking money from the till and he was taken to the police station. After several hours' questioning, he confessed that he had stolen the money. But before the case came to court, his employer discovered that Mohammed was innocent: the money had been banked, and had never been stolen at all.

Colin Lattimore, who is mentally subnormal, was arrested on suspicion of murder. He was 17 when this happened. He was questioned for nine hours in the police station, without his parents or anyone other than the police being present. He signed a confession statement admitting the murder. It was later proved that the murder took place at a time when Colin had an undisputed alibi: although he was innocent, he had been pressured into signing a false confession. He spent three years in prison before the truth was established.

Your rights

In addition to not having to answer questions or make a statement, you have a number of other rights at the police station. These are:

1. If you are under 17, the police must inform your parents or guardian of your arrest.

2. In addition, everyone who has been arrested has the right to have someone told of their arrest and where they are being held. You should tell the officer who arrested you or the sergeant at the desk who you want told (your parents, a friend, a lawyer or social worker) and give their phone number or address. The police should not delay in contacting them any longer than is necessary.

3. The right to contact a solicitor and talk to him/her privately. In theory, you should be allowed to do this at any stage of the investigation. But the police can refuse to let you contact a solicitor if it would 'unreasonably hinder' their investigations. In practice, you

probably won't be allowed to see a solicitor until you have been charged.

4. If you are under 17, you should only be interviewed if your parents or a teacher, social worker or another adult of the same sex as you is present. This rule is often broken and you may need to remind the police of it.

5. The right to be made reasonably comfortable and to be offered refreshments.

Although these rights are laid down in the Judges Rules, which the police are meant to follow, they are often ignored.

Being charged

If you are under 17, the police will usually wait until your parents have arrived before charging you, even if your parents weren't allowed to be there while you were questioned. Being charged with an offence means that you will be tried in a court (see chapter 9 for more on the criminal courts).

When you are charged, the officer will caution you again. You will be asked if you want to say anything and again you don't have to. It is probably better to say nothing at this stage. After you have been charged, the police should not question you any more about what you are meant to have done. But they will probably ask you about your background, school, exam results and so on, and note down details of your physical appearance.

Fingerprints and photographs

If you are under 14, the police cannot take your fingerprints unless your parents consent. If they do consent, your fingerprints may remain on the police file – even if you are only cautioned, or even if you are acquitted (found innocent) of the offence. If they don't consent, there is nothing the police can do to force you to give your prints.

If you are aged 14 or over you don't have to give your fingerprints. If you refuse, the police can apply to the magistrates for permission to take them anyway. But if your fingerprints are taken under a court order, and you are later acquitted of the offence, then you have a right to have the fingerprints destroyed. There is a risk though that the police may keep you in the station overnight if they have to go to court for a fingerprinting order. If you agree to be finger-printed without a court order being made, you have no right to insist on having the prints destroyed even if you are acquitted.

If you are held under the Prevention of Terrorism Act or the

Immigration Act (which occasionally happens to young people), you have to give your fingerprints and let the police take your photo. As a general rule, the police will take your photo at the police station. But if you refuse, they have no right to force you to be photographed.

How long can you be held by the police?

If you are under 14, you must be released from the police station as soon as the police have completed their enquiries. If they want to keep you longer, they have to apply for a place of safety order (see page 42) which allows you to be held for up to eight days. They can do this if they suspect you of a very serious offence, or if they think you will be at risk if you go home — for instance, your parents may hit you.

If you are aged 14, 15 or 16, you must be given bail after you are charged with a criminal offence. Bail means that you go free until the day set for you to appear in court. You can only be refused bail if a senior police officer believes that:

— you have nowhere to go or you would be harmed if you went home;
— you will not appear in court if you are released;
— you have committed a serious crime such as murder or manslaughter;
— you would interfere with the police case against you, eg by frightening police witnesses or tipping off other people involved who haven't yet been caught.

The police can insist that your parents enter into a 'recognisance' for you. This means they pledge a certain sum of money, which they will lose if you do not appear at court on the day you are told to.

If the police refuse you bail, you must be kept in a 'place of safety' (usually a local authority home) until your trial. But if you are a boy and the police certify that you are 'unruly' you may be sent to a remand centre, run like a prison, or — if there are no remand centre places — to an adult prison.

The police then have to bring you to the juvenile court within 72 hours (three days) unless a senior police officer certifies that you are too ill to attend.

At the court, either you, your lawyer or your parents should apply for bail so that you don't go on having to stay in detention before your case is heard. (See page 93 for more on what happens at the court).

Making a note of what happened to you

If you have ever been in court, you may have noticed that police officers are allowed to refer to their note-books when they give evidence – provided they convince the magistrates that the notes were made at the time, or shortly after the incident.

You also have the right to use your notes to help you remember what happened when you were arrested and held by the police.

It can be months before your case is heard by the court and most people's memories fade quickly. So it is a great help if you are able to write down what happened at the time – either in the police station if the police let you have paper and a pen, or as soon as possible after you are released.

If possible, try and write down what the police said and did; the name and number, if you know them, of the officers involved; what the police asked you and what you said (use the exact words as closely as you remember); what they took when they searched you or your home; what offence they said you were being charged with. Put the time and date at the bottom, and sign it.

Any notes you make at the time will be very useful for your lawyer. If you don't have a lawyer, you should take your notes along to the court with you, and ask the magistrates for permission to use them to refresh your memory of what happened.

Jumping bail

If you don't appear at court when you are meant to, then the juvenile court will probably issue a warrant for your arrest. It is an offence not to 'surrender to bail' (i.e. not to come to court after being released on bail).

Being cautioned by the police

If the police suspect you of committing a fairly trivial offence and you haven't been in serious trouble before, the police may refer you to the **Juvenile Bureau**. This is run by plain-clothes police.

Juvenile Bureaux differ from area to area, but basically they decide whether or not you are going to be prosecuted or just cautioned. They will take account of your home background, your school record and what the crime is that you're supposed to have committed. They usually talk to your parents, teachers and social workers. If there is very little evidence against you, the Bureau will probably decide that nothing should be done. If the reports they receive about you are bad, they will probably decide to prosecute. Otherwise, they will caution you.

Being cautioned means that you will have to admit committing the offence and you and your parents will have to go the police station to listen to a stern telling-off from a senior police officer. Although a caution does not count as a conviction it may be mentioned in court if you appear there in future charged with another offence. For this reason, you should not agree to be cautioned if you have a defence to the accusation.

Helping someone who is being held by the police

If your child, or someone in your care, is being held by the police, you should be notified. (See page 81 for when an arrested person can have someone told of his/her arrest). If you haven't been told but think that someone you know is being detained, you should try to find out where they are by phoning round the local police stations (in the phone book under 'police').

If you are the parent of someone held by the police (or a social worker or teacher involved with the arrested person), you should go down to the police station and ask to be allowed in during police questioning. No-one under 17 should be questioned without a parent or another adult of the same sex as the arrested person being present. If this is refused, you should make a formal complaint against the police.

You should also contact a solicitor or legal advice agency, to arrange for a lawyer to be present when the person who has been arrested is brought up in court. See page 92.

You may find that you get no help from the police you speak to, and that everyone denies having heard of the person you think has been arrested. Someone from an advice agency, or a solicitor, can help here and may get more co-operation from the police than you do.

Complaints against the police

You can make a complaint to the chief officer of police for the area. In London, he is called the Commissioner of Police; outside London, he is called the Chief Constable. He has to appoint an investigator (usually from an outside force or, in London, from a different division) to investigate your complaint. The chief police officer then decides whether or not to take disciplinary action against the policeman you complained about. In a serious case, the investigator's report goes to the Director of Public Prosecutions who decides whether the police officer should be prosecuted.

There is also an independent Police Complaints Board, which

has to receive a report of the outcome of all complaints and occasionally intervenes in a serious case.

You should make your complaint in writing, directly to the chief officer, or via the Police Complaints Board, Waterloo Bridge House, London SE1 (01-275 3072). Keep a copy of the complaint, and ask for a copy of the statement you make to the investigating officer.

If the police are prosecuting you for a criminal offence, and you also want to make a complaint about the way they behaved, you should discuss this with your solicitor first. Your complaint will probably not be investigated until after the case against you is heard.

You can get a leaflet about police complaints from the police station. NCCL also publish a fact sheet on police complaints, as part of a series on people's rights and the police (50p from 186 Kings Cross Road, London WC1).

If you are a witness to a crime

If, for instance, you see a car accident or if you are a witness to a robbery or mugging, the police may want to question you to help them get evidence. They may simply take your name and address and contact you later. Or they may ask you to go to the police station immediately to give a statement. In order to do their job, the police need the co-operation of witnesses.

If you are under 17 and the police want to interview you as a witness, they should only do so if one of your parents or a teacher or your social worker or another adult of the same sex as you is present. You should tell them who you want to be present.

Witnesses have the same rights as people suspected of crimes. You don't have to answer questions or make a statement if you don't want to. Anything you do say can be used in evidence against the person who is eventually charged with the criminal offence. If what you say makes the police suspicious of you, it could be used to bring a prosecution against you.

Occasionally, witnesses are bullied by the police to say what the police want. Moussa, a 16-year-old boy, came to the NCCL after he had been kept in the police station for three days. He wasn't suspected of anything — but the police wanted him to make a statement about someone he knew who was suspected of murder. Eventually he gave the police the statement they wanted (although he says the statement was false), in order to get out of the police station. He claims the police said they would prosecute him for perjury if he didn't tell them what they wanted to know.

If you think the police are beginning to suspect you, or if you think they're behaving unfairly, you should not say anything more to them until you have talked to a lawyer yourself.

86

Reporting a crime to the police

If you have been attacked or robbed, you will probably want to report it to the police. You should contact the local police station (in the phone book under 'police') as soon as possible. There's no point in telling the police days after it happened: your memory of what happened won't be so good, and they probably won't be able to do much by then anyway.

The police will take details about you and about what happened. They will ask you for any information which might help identify the person who did the crime. Most people have very bad memories for people's faces and appearance, so it is important to tell the police only what you remember clearly and not to exaggerate.

If you have been raped, or sexually attacked or had a man expose himself to you, the police may be suspicious of your story. An article in the *Police Review* warned police officers that children and women complaining of sexual crimes might be lying in order to get someone into trouble or draw attention to themselves. But the police should be told of the attack, if possible immediately, at least in order to protect others. If you are the victim of a sex offence, you should only be questioned by a police officer who is the same sex as you.

The Rape Crisis Centre helps victims of sexual attacks. You can contact them on 01-340 6145 (24-hour phone) or 01-340 6913 (office hours) or write to PO Box 42, London N6 5BU.

Victims of crime can apply for compensation to the Criminal Injuries Compensation Board, 10-12 Russell Square, London WC1 (01-636 2812).

9

THE JUVENILE COURT

The juvenile court deals with cases involving people under 17. This includes both criminal cases, where you are charged with an offence, and care hearings where the court has to decide whether or not the local council should take you into care. Care proceedings are dealt with in chapter 3. *This chapter deals with criminal cases at the juvenile court.*

There are usually three **magistrates** at the juvenile court. Most magistrates are local people appointed to hear cases; they are given some training, but rely heavily on the advice of the court clerk who is usually a lawyer. In some big cities, a full-time magistrate who is a lawyer sits on his own to hear all cases; he is called a **stipendiary** or 'stipe'.

There is no jury or judge at the juvenile court, although in some cases the juvenile court can decide to refer you to the Crown Court for the trial or to be sentenced. The Crown Court consists of a judge and a jury, although there will only be a judge if you have simply been referred to the court for sentence.

Juvenile courts are meant to be informal, but vary a lot in practice. Some are held in vast Victorian buildings, others in much smaller, modern buildings with fitted carpets and ordinary chairs. Some juvenile courts are in the same building as the adult magistrates' court. But the law says that if a juvenile court is to be held in a room which is also used as a court where adults are tried, then there must be at least one hour's gap between the two cases!

When young people can be tried in adult courts

The normal rule is that people under the age of 17 must be tried in the juvenile court. You cannot choose to be tried by a jury. But in some cases you may be sent either to the adult magistrates' court or to the Crown Court, where trials are heard by a judge and jury.

If a juvenile court is to be held in the same room as an adult court at least one hour must elapse between the two.

You can be tried by an adult court if:

1. You are being charged with a criminal offence together with an adult. If you are under 17 and the other person is 17 or over then your case has to be dealt with by the adult magistrates' court. This could happen, for instance, if you are both accused with stealing something from a shop. But if you are charged just with *helping* the other person to commit the offence, then the magistrates might decide to send you to the juvenile court instead.

If you are tried at the magistrates' court, and you are found guilty you will usually be sent back to the juvenile court for sentencing. (See page 95 for more on sentencing.)

2. You are being charged with an adult, and either he or the police decide to have the case heard by a jury at the Crown Court. Some offences can be tried either at the magistrates' court or at the Crown Court, while serious offence (eg murder, rape, robbery) can only be dealt with by the Crown Court. If the other person is being tried at the Crown Court, both you and he will probably be tried together there. But if you plead not guilty you could be sent back to the juvenile court for trial.

3. You are charged with murder, manslaughter, causing death by dangerous driving or any other offence involving killing someone. In this case, you must be tried at the Crown Court.

4. If you are charged with a very serious offence, for which an adult could be sent to prison for 14 years or more, you can be tried by the Crown Court. The court will only decide to send you to the Crown Court if they think that, if you are found guilty, you would need to be detained for a long time.

Summons

A prosecution in a criminal case can begin either with an arrest, or with a summons. A summons is a notice ordering you to turn up at court on a particular day. If you don't obey the summons, the case may be put off to another day, or a warrant will be issued for your arrest. If there is some reason why you can't go to court — for instance, because you're ill — let the court know.

If you haven't time to get a lawyer and prepare your case before the date given on the summons, write to the court asking them to change the date. Alternatively, go along on the day and ask for an **adjournment** (i.e. a delay before the case is heard) to give you more time. If you don't hear from the court giving you a new date, you must still turn up on the date notified.

Arrest

Chapter 8 sets out the powers the police have to arrest you. If you were released on bail by the police, you will have been told what day to come to court. If you don't turn up at court, the magistrates will probably give the police a warrant for your arrest.

For a serious offence, the police might arrange for you to be kept in custody overnight and take you to the juvenile court the next day. If this happens, ask for an adjournment so that you have time to get a lawyer and prepare your case. You should also ask for bail, so that you can return home instead of being kept in a local council home or remand centre before the trial. Finally, you should ask for legal aid to pay for the lawyer. More about bail on page 91, and legal aid on page 92.

Delays in hearing your case

It is very common in London, and some other big cities, for cases to be repeatedly adjourned so that by the time your case is heard months may have passed since the original incident. This makes it very hard for you or the witnesses to remember what actually happened. It helps if you see a lawyer as soon as possible, so that he has a statement from you while the events are still fresh in your mind. It is also very helpful if you wrote down a note of what happened while you were at the police station or very soon after you left.

Getting help with your case

It is very important to get advice from a solicitor about your case, even if you intend to plead guilty. You need to find out whether you have a defence to the case (since the law is so technical, you may in fact be innocent without realising it). Even if you are guilty, you may need a solicitor to explain to the court why you should be dealt with lightly — this is called a 'speech in mitigation'. If you are convicted or given a heavy sentence you should get legal advice about the possibility of an appeal.

Many people only realise they should have had a lawyer or pleaded 'not guilty' after it's all over. By then it's too late — you need to get a lawyer as quickly as possible. (See page 92.)

The police may tell you 'It's easier to get it over with.' It may be for them — but not for you.

Bail

If the court cannot hear your case on the day you appear, they can adjourn or **remand** it to another day. The magistrates will normally give you bail, which means you can go free until the date set for the next hearing. The court should only refuse you bail if it is satisfied that:

— you would not come back to court for your case; or

— you would commit offences while on bail; or

— you would interfere with witnesses or obstruct the course of justice; or

— it is in your own interests to be kept in custody.

If you have been found guilty and the magistrates decide to get reports (e.g. from social workers) about you before sentencing you, they should also give you bail unless they think that it would be impractical to make the report if you are on bail.

If the court gives you bail, they can also impose conditions — for instance, that you stay away from certain places or don't go out after a certain time at night. They can also ask for **sureties**: people willing to pledge a certain sum of money which they will probably forfeit if you don't turn up at court. Your parents are usually asked to stand surety and can be asked to pledge up to £50.

91

It is an offence not to turn up at court after being given bail, and the court can then issue a warrant for your arrest.

If the court refuses to grant you bail, they must remand you into the care of the local authority until your case comes to court again. You will probably be sent to a community home. A girl can be placed in a 'secure unit' of a community home if they think you will run away. But a boy will be sent to a remand centre or even a prison if the court makes what is called a **'certificate of unruliness'**.

If the court feels that you are so unruly a character that you can't safely be committed to the care of the local council, then it can make an unruliness certificate, provided that:

— you are charged with an offence for which an adult could be sent to prison for more than 14 years (e.g. homicide, rape); or

— you have been charged with an offence of violence and have been found guilty of an offence of violence on a previous occasion; or

— you have persistently run away from a community home or seriously disrupted the running of a community home, and the court is satisfied on the basis of the local council's report that there is no community home you could be sent to without the risk of your disrupting it or running away.

Where either of the first two conditions applies, the local council also have to tell the court that there is no suitable community home for you, before the court can make an unruliness certificate. If it is the first time that your case has been remanded, then the court can do without the local council report if it is satisfied that there hasn't been enough time to prepare it.

If the court makes an unruliness certificate and has been told that there is a **remand centre** available (e.g. Ashford in Middlesex or Risley near Manchester), then it can send you to the centre for up to 28 days. Remand centres are run by the Home Office who run the prisons, and are organised along similar lines. If no remand centre place is available, you could be sent to a prison.

If you are remanded in care, or certified as unruly, you can apply to a High Court judge for bail. You should consult a solicitor for help with this.

Lawyers and legal aid

If you don't know a solicitor, you can get a list from the court or the local Citizens Advice Bureau (look in the phone book). Or a friend may be able to suggest a solicitor. If there is a law centre in your area (in the phone book or ask the CAB), they can help either by representing you or giving you the name of good local solicitors.

Some juvenile courts (including most in Inner London) have a **duty solicitor scheme**, which means that there is always a solicitor at court who will see you, give you advice and, if necessary, represent you. Some juvenile courts share solicitors with the local adult magistrates court. You can ask about this when you get to court: an official or the court officer will tell you.

If you haven't got a solicitor by the time you get to court, don't be afraid to ask the court to adjourn your case to another date to give you a chance to find one. If you go to court without a lawyer and are found guilty and perhaps given a severe punishment, it will be too late afterwards to wish you had got legal advice. You cannot appeal against the court's decision just because you were unrepresented.

If you go to a solicitor, you will probably be entitled to legal aid to cover his costs. Ask the solicitor about this and get him/her to fill in the forms. Alternatively, you can get the forms from the court, fill them in and get the court to allocate you a solicitor. This is useful if you don't know of any solicitors, although it is obviously better to find a good solicitor who specialises in criminal cases, rather than just having the court pick one out for you. If you are aged under 16, your parents should sign the legal aid form for you, although you can get legal aid even without their signature. If you are in care, your social worker will sign the form.

Who will be at the court hearing?

The public are not allowed to attend the juvenile court. Only the magistrates and court officers, people involved in the case and newspaper reporters are allowed to be present. Anyone else wanting to attend has to get special permission. This is different from the magistrates' court where almost anyone can attend.

Newspaper reporters aren't allowed to print your name or address or the name of your school, or a photo or anything else which would tell people who you are. This applies if you are a witness in a case, as well as if you are actually being charged wth an offence. Occasionally, however, the magistrates allow your name to be published — for instance, if you are a witness but there are rumours going round that you are the person charged with a crime.

What happens at the hearing

You and your parents sit on the row of chairs immediately in front of the magistrates. Your lawyers will usually sit to one side. Other people, like probation officers, educational welfare workers and social workers sit at the back or on the other side. People giving evidence stand in a witness box on one side of the courtroom.

Most people who appear in court are far too worried or confused to notice much about the other people in the court or who everyone is. But the magistrates are supposed to help you understand what's going on. Here is an outline of what will happen.

1. Either the magistrates or the clerk to the court should explain the charge to you in simple language.

2. The magistrate asks you whether or not you admit committing the offence. If you admit it, the magistrates will then decide what to do about you (as in points 8 and 9 on page 95).

3. If you deny doing the offence, you say 'Not guilty' or 'I didn't do it' or something like that. The magistrates then go on to hear the evidence against you and your defence. They always begin by hearing the prosecution. The police officer or a solicitor employed by the police usually starts by briefly explaining what they think you did. They then call each of their witnesses – for instance, the police officer who arrested you; or the shopkeeper who says you stole from his shop; or the person who claims you tried to rob him; or the person whose car you are accused of having taken away.

4. You or your parents or your lawyer have the right to question each of the witnesses after they have finished answering the police questions. This is called **cross-examination**. The magistrates may also ask questions.

5. When the police have finished their case, the magistrates will hear your side of the story. You or your parents or your lawyer can start by explaining to the court why you deny doing the offence. Then you will probably give evidence yourself, by going into the witness box and explaining your side of the story by answering the questions your lawyer or the clerk or magistrates ask. You can then call witnesses – for instance, someone who was with you at the time the offence was committed and who can show that you were in a different place from where the offence happened (this is called an **alibi**). The police lawyer can cross-examine your witnesses after you or your lawyer have finished questioning them. You do not have to give evidence yourself or call witnesses; talk to your lawyer about this.

6. If your lawyer, or you or your parents did not make a speech at the beginning of your case (point 5), you can do so now. Occasionally the magistrates allow you and the police to make final speeches, in addition to the opening ones – but this is rare.

7. Now that they have heard all the evidence, the magistrates decide whether or not they think you are guilty. They often go into a back room to discuss the case before giving their verdict. If they say you are not guilty (**acquitted**), that's the end of the matter.

8. If they decide you are guilty, or if you admitted the offence in the first place, they have to decide what sentence to give you. Before deciding this, the magistrates may want to see reports written by social workers, teachers, a probation officer or a doctor about you or your family. (More about reports below.) They may adjourn the case again and sentence you on a future date (see page 91 on bail).

9. The different **sentences** which you could be given are set out in detail below — ranging from an absolute discharge to a stretch in borstal for a serious offence.

Taking the oath

Everyone who gives evidence has to promise the court that they will tell the truth. This is called taking the **oath** or affirming. If you take the oath you have to hold the Bible, Koran or Bhagavita, depending on your religion. Affirming is for people who don't have a religious belief.

If the magistrates think you are too young to understand the nature of the oath, they may allow you to give evidence anyway provided they think you understand that you have to tell the truth.

Court reports

In many courts, you, your parents or your lawyer will be given a copy of any report shown to the magistrates. Unfortunately not all courts do this and many social workers still object to it. In any event, the magistrates either have to read the report out aloud or else they have to summarise the sections of the report which have influenced their decision. Although the law says they have to do this, they don't always. You can't insist on seeing the report — but you can insist on being told the relevant bits of it.

Previous convictions

Before deciding what sentence to give you, the magistrates also hear about any other offences for which you have been convicted. Usually these are read out by the police officer. If you have been cautioned (see page 82), this can also be referred to by the officer.

Sentences

There are many different sentences which a court can decide on. We set them out briefly below.

1. Absolute discharge

This means that you are technically found guilty – but you don't have to pay a fine or serve a borstal sentence or anything else. It usually means that the magistrates think that the police should not have prosecuted you or that it would be unfair to punish you.

2. Conditional discharge

This is also a conviction without a punishment. But it can be held over you for up to three years. If you are convicted of another offence in that time, you can be given a punishment for the first offence as well as for the new one.

3. Fine

You can be ordered to pay a fine. The maximum amount of fine for any particular offence is fixed by law. The magistrates have to take into account how much money you have in deciding what sum to fine you. If you're under 17, you can't be fined more than £200. Occasionally, the magistrates may order your parents to pay the fine instead of you. If you don't pay up, you may be ordered to go to an attendance centre (see point 5 below) – or your parents could be ordered to pay instead.

4. Compensation Order

The magistrates can order you to pay up to £400 compensation to the victim of your crime. For instance, if you are convicted of burglary you could be ordered to pay the cost of replacing the window you broke in order to get in, as well as the cost of the goods you stole if these have not been got back.

A compensation order may be the only punishment you get, or it may be in addition to, say, a supervision order or one of the other sentences mentioned in this list. If you don't pay the compensation, a social worker may be asked to supervise you or you can be sent to an attendance centre.

5. Being disqualified from driving

The juvenile court can disqualify you from driving or holding a driving licence – even if you are too young to have a licence anyway. You will almost always be disqualified, in addition to any other sentence you may get, if you are convicted of taking and driving away another person's car ('TDA').

6. Attendance Centre

These are meant to provide a 'short, sharp punishment'.

You can be ordered to go to an attendance centre if:

– if you have been found guilty of an offence for which an adult could be sent to prison (including most offences involving theft or violence); *and*

– you have not been sentenced to borstal training or detention (see points 9 and 10 below); *and*

– there is an attendance centre near enough for you to get to.

The magistrates will order you to go to the attendance centre for a set number of times. The total is usually 12 hours but can be less if you are under 14, or up to 24 hours if the court thinks that 12 isn't enough.

The magistrates will tell you which dates you have to go to the attendance centre. The sessions are usually held on Saturday afternoons and you will normally have to do physical training there.

If you don't turn up at the attendance centre, or you break its rules, you can be brought back to the court which can send you to a detention centre or impose any of the other sentences mentioned in this list.

7. Supervision Order

This means that a social worker will supervise you for up to three years. S/he is meant to be able to advise and help you by keeping in regular touch with you. You are meant to co-operate with the social worker and see him/her regularly.

Sometimes the magistrates will attach conditions to the supervision order, e.g:

– to live at a particular place (usually with your parents);

– to inform your social worker immediately of any change of address or job;

– to keep in touch with the social worker;

– if the social worker wants, to let him/her visit you at home;

– to 'be of good behaviour';

– to go to school.

Conditions can only be imposed if you agree (or, if you are under 14, your parents agree). If you break these conditions you can be fined up to £50 or ordered to go to an attendance centre (see point 5 above).

As part of a supervision order, the court can order that you take part in an **intermediate treatment** scheme for up to 30 days in each year that the supervision order lasts. It is up to your social worker to decide whether or not to implement the order. Intermediate treatment schemes vary but often involve group activities such as helping at youth clubs and adventure playgrounds, or taking part in sports, evening classes, handicrafts and so on.

If you don't co-operate with the supervision order, the local authority may apply to the court to stop the supervision order and have you taken into care instead.

A supervision order imposed after you have been found guilty of an offence lasts up to three years (although it cannot last beyond your 20th birthday). If you are aged 18 or over and don't obey the supervision order, the local council can apply to the adult magistrates' court to have the order varied (e.g. by changing the conditions attached to the order) or cancelled. If you have broken the terms of the order, the court could decide to send you to an attendance centre, fine you up to £1000 or even send you to prison for up to six months instead.

A supervision order made in care proceedings (see page 42) has to end when you turn 18.

You can apply to have the supervision order ended. You might find it helpful to get advice from a solicitor about this.

8. Binding over

Very occasionally, the magistrates may decide to bind either you or your parents over. This means that your parents have to pledge a sum of money up to £200 (called a 'recognisance') as a promise that they will take proper care over you and control you properly. If they don't manage to do this, and for instance you are later found guilty of another offence, they forfeit their money.

9. Care order

A care order means that the local council takes over the rights and duties of your parents, and can insist on your living in a community home. A care order normally lasts until you are 18. But if you are aged 16 or 17 when it is made it lasts until you are 19.

A care order can be made if you are found guilty of an offence for which an adult could be imprisoned (e.g. most offences involving theft and violence or taking and driving away a vehicle).

See chapter 3 for detailed information on care.

10. Detention Centre

If you are aged 14 or over, and you are found guilty of an offence for which an adult could be imprisoned, you can be sent to a detention centre. This applies to boys only – there are no detention centres for girls.

98

Detention centres emphasise hard physical activity rather than education.

Six weeks is the usual length of time spent at a detention centre, although you can be sentenced to up to three months.

Detention centres are meant to provide a 'short, sharp shock' in order to put you off a life of crime before you have acquired a serious criminal record. They are run on strict lines with an emphasis on hard physical activity. Because they are not suitable for someone who is physically or mentally unfit, the court has to get a medical report on you first.

When you leave a detention centre, you will be supervised by a probation officer or social worker for up to 12 months.

11. Borstal

You can be sent to a borstal for between six months and two years if you are aged between 15 and 20 and convicted of an offence for which an adult could be sentenced to prison. Both girls and boys can be sent to borstal, although there are separate borstals for each sex.

With one exception, borstal is the heaviest sentence for a young person and the juvenile magistrates cannot impose the sentence themselves. They have to refer you to the Crown Court, with a recommendation for borstal training. Until the Crown Court hears your case, you can be sent to a remand centre or prison, or released on bail (see page 91).

At the Crown Court, you or your lawyer can make a speech to the court explaining the circumstances of the offence and perhaps urging them to consider an alternative to borstal.

The idea behind borstal is that taking you away from your home, placing you in a borstal for several months, and giving you training there will result in you becoming a reformed character. Unfortunately, a very large number of people sent to borstal later commit offences after release. Although there are many reasons for this, one is that the quality of training and education in borstals is very low. Borstals have been widely criticised in recent years, and some people want to see them abolished. Indeed, the Younger Report on young adult offenders recommended their abolition.

You can also be sent to borstal by the juvenile court if you are over 15 and are resident in a community home under a care order where the local authority feel that you ought to be transferred to borstal. In such circumstances the local authority has to get the consent of the Secretary of State to bring you before the juvenile court. If the court is satisfied that your behaviour is such that your presence in any community home will be harmful to others living there, then it can order you to be sent to borstal. When that happens the care order ceases to have any effect and you are treated as if you had been sentenced to borstal from the date on which the order was made. Such orders are extremely rare.

After you leave borstal, you can be supervised by a probation officer or social worker for up to two years. If you are convicted of an offence while you are under supervision, then you can be recalled to borstal – and kept there until two years after the date when the first borstal sentence was imposed.

12. Deferred sentence

The court can put off (i.e. defer) passing sentence on you, to see how you behave for the next few months. Sentence can only be deferred for a maximum of six months, and you have to agree. If you keep out of trouble in that time, the court will take this into account when you come back to be sentenced: but equally, if you commit other offences, they may give you a more severe punishment for the original offence.

13. Hospital or guardianship order

If a young person under the age of 17 is convicted of an offence for which an adult could be imprisoned, and two doctors certify that s/he is suffering from mental illness, psychopathic disorder, subnormality or severe subnormality, the court may order him or her to be detained in mental hospital. Alternatively, the court may order the local authority to become the person's guardian. If the magistrates think that there should be restrictions on the person's release from hospital, they have to refer the case to the Crown Court which can make a hospital order saying that s/he can only be released with the Home Secretary's consent.

14. Prison

As a general rule, you can't be sent to prison if you are under 17. (in practice, some young people go to prison *before* trial, as we explained on page 92).

If you are aged between 17 and 21, you can only be sent to prison for six months or less or − for a more serious offence − for three years or more.

15. Detention subject to the directions of the Home Secretary

If you are convicted of a very serious offence, for which an adult could be sent to prison for 14 years or more − for instance, homicide, rape, robbery or burglary − then the court can order you to be detained 'subject to the direction of the Secretary of State'. This means that you are detained on whatever conditions he decides. At first, this will probably be in a borstal, community home or a youth treatment unit designed to deal with very disturbed children. But after you become an adult, you will probably be transferred to prison.

Legal costs

If you are found guilty, the magistrates may order you to pay part of the costs of the police in bringing the prosecution. If you don't pay, you can be sent to an attendance centre instead (see point 6 above). Your own lawyer should be paid for out of legal aid (see page 92).

10
COMING OF AGE:
A SUMMARY OF YOUR RIGHTS YEAR BY YEAR

We set out here a summary of your rights year by year. We've put in as much as possible, but we can't cover everything! More information on most of the points mentioned is given in other chapters.

You . . .

can have an account in your name with a bank or building society, or have Premium Bonds in your name.

must go to school or other full-time education;
can drink alcohol legally in private.

can:

draw money from your Post Office or TSB savings account;
go to an A film without an adult.

can be convicted of a criminal offence (but until you are 14, the prosecution has to prove you know the difference between right and wrong).

can buy a pet without a parent being present.

can get a part-time job so long as it is a 'light' one for not more than two hours per day or one on Sundays.

can:

be held fully responsible for a crime;
be sent to a detention centre, if convicted of a crime;
own an air rifle and, under certain conditions, a shot-gun;
see an AA film;
go into a pub, but not drink or buy alcohol there;
play dominoes or cribbage in a pub;
be fingerprinted if you agree or if a magistrate orders your prints to be taken;
pawn goods in a pawn shop;
be found guilty of rape (boys);
must pay full fare on public transport.

can:

be sent to borstal;
be sent to prison to await trial (boys).

can:

leave school;
get a full-time job and join a union;
marry with the consent of one parent, your guardian or the court;
leave home with a parent's consent;
consent to sexual intercourse (girls);
claim supplementary and social security benefits;
drink beer, wine, cider or perry in a pub, hotel or restaurant if you're having a meal;
buy cigarettes or tobacco;
choose your own doctor and consent to medical treatment;
hold a licence to drive a moped, motor-cycle, certain tractors and invalid carriages;
get a passport with your parent's signature on the application form;
choose your own religion;
buy fireworks and Premium bonds;
enter a brothel and live there;
sell scrap metal;
have to pay prescription charges.
join the armed forces with your parents' consent (boys).

can:

go into a betting shop, but not bet;
become a street trader;
join the armed forces with your parents' consent (girls);
hold a driving licence for all types of vehicles except heavy goods vehicles;
be sent to prison if you are convicted of a serious crime.

can:

leave home whether or not your parents agree;

marry without your parents' consent;

join the armed forces without your parents' consent:

vote and sit on a jury:

get a cheque card and credit card;

see an X film;

make a will and act as executor for someone's else's will;

give blood;

change your name without your parent's consent;

apply for your own passport;

buy on HP, get credit and a mortgage;

own land, property and shares in your own name;

sign contracts, sue and be sued in the courts;

buy drinks in pubs and drink them there;

work in a bar;

bet;

see your birth certificate if you are adopted.

have to pay for dental treatment.

can:

stand for the local council or Parliament;

adopt a child;

engage in homosexual activity in private, if you are a man and your partner is a consenting man aged 21 or over;

hold a licence to sell intoxicating liquor;

be sentenced to life imprisonment if convicted of certain very serious crimes;

hold a licence to drive a lorry or a bus.

USEFUL BOOKS AND PAMPHLETS

In addition to the books mentioned at the end of each section in this guide, you may find the following helpful.

Civil Liberty: The NCCL Guide, edited by Grant and others; comprehensive guide to the law and your rights (Penguin, 1979, £1.75)

The Little Red Schoolbook, by Soren and Jasper Jensen. There was an attempt by the authorities to ban this book, and parts of it have been cut. Clear, useful information, particularly about school. (Stage 1, 1971, 30p)

Make It Happy: What Sex is All About, by Jane Cousins. Easy-to-read, sensible, non-sexist. (Virago, £2.95)

Rights: A Handbook for People Under Age, by Nan Berger. Interesting, well illustrated book with practical information and points for discussion (Penguin 1974, 60p)

The Single Woman's Guide to Pregnancy and Parenthood, by Patricia Ashdown-Sharp. Very useful, practical guide for both sexes. (Penguin 1975, 95p)

Teachers and the Law, by G R Barrell. Legal handbook for teachers on employment law, schools, juvenile court etc. Useful for young people as well as teachers. (Methuen, 1978, £6.95)

Trouble with the Law, The Release Bust Book: practical advice on police powers, courts, lawyers, etc. (Pluto Press, 1978, £1.25)

Women's Rights: A Practical Guide, by Anna Coote and Tess Gill. Extremely useful guide covering sex discrimination and equal pay, social security, law on sex, marriage, motherhood, cohabitation etc. Useful for men too. (Penguin, 1978, £1.25)

SCOTLAND

Your Rights at the Children's hearings; SCCL; 12p each, special rates for bulk order.

Children's Rights: Extinction or Rebirth? SCCL; £1.10

Your Rights in Scotland: The SCCL Guide (forthcoming)

Legality and Community: The Politics of Juvenile Justice in Scotland; Aberdeen Peoples's Press, £1.75

USEFUL ORGANISA- TIONS

You can get more information about these organisations, including a list of their publications, by writing to them with a stamped addressed envelope.

Abortion Law Reform Association 88A Islington High Street, London N1 (01-359 5200); campaigning organisation, does not give advice.

Adoption Resource Exchange 40 Brunswick Square, London WC1 (01-837 0496); specialises in finding homes for children with special needs.

Advisory Centre for Education (ACE) 18 Victoria Park Square, London EC2 (01-980 4596)

Advisory Service for Squatters 2 St Paul's Road, London N1 (01-359 8814; hours 12-6)

After Six Housing Advisory Service Trust 48 William IV Street, London WC2 (01-836 6534)

Alone in London Service 190 Euston Road, London NW1 (01-387 3010); advice and practical help for single young women and men. Near Euston Station.

Albany Trust 16-20 Strutton Ground, London SW1 (01-222 0701); advises on sexual problems.

Alcoholics Anonymous 11 Redcliffe Gardens, London SW10 (general enquiries 01-352 9779; practical advice in Greater London 01-834 8202; for local numbers, see local phone book)

Amnesty International, 10 Southampton Street, London WC2 (01-836 7788)

Apex Trust 31-3 Clapham Road, London SW9 (01-592 3171); helps ex-prisoners find jobs.

Association of British Adoption and Fostering Agencies 4 Southampton Row, London WC1 (01-242 8951)

British Association for Counselling 26 Bedford Square, London WC1 (01-636 4066); can provide list of local counselling and advisory centres (please send 90p).

British Pregnancy Advisory Service Guildhall Buildings, Navigation Street, Birmingham 2 (021-643 1461) or 58 Petty France, London SW1 (01-222 0985).

British Youth Council 57 Chalton Street, London NW1 (01-387 7559)

Brook Advisory Centre 233 Tottenham Court Road, London W1 (01-580 2991, 01-323 1522); advice and help on contraception, pregnancy, abortion; particularly designed to help young people.

Campaign for Homosexual Equality (CHE) PO Box 427, 69 Corporation Street, Manchester M60 2EZ (061-228 1985)

Centrepoint 65A Shaftesbury Avenue, London W1 (night shelter for people aged 16-25 who are new to London; open 8pm-8am every day)

Child Poverty Action Group 1 Macklin Street, London WC2 (01-242 3225)

Citizen's Advice Bureaux (National Association), 110 Drury Lane, London WC2 (01-836 9231); look in phone book for local CAB

Citizens' Rights Office 1 Macklin Street, London WC2 (01-405 5942); advice and help on social security problems

Commission for Racial Equality 10-12 Allington Street, London SW1 (01-828 7022)

Confederation for the Advancement of State Education (CASE) c/o 81 Rustings Road, Sheffield 11 (0742-662467)

Department of Education and Science Elizabeth House, York Road, London SE1 (01-928 9222)

Drugs Information Advisory Service 111 Cowbridge Road East, Canton, Cardiff (0222-26113)

Equal Opportunities Commission Overseas House, Quay Street, Manchester (061-833 9244)

Family Planning Association of Northern Ireland 47 Botanic Avenue, Belfast 7 (0232-25488)

Family Planning Information Service 27 Mortimer Street, London W1 (01-636 7866)

Family Rights Group 24 Romilly Road, London N4

Gay Switchboard c/o 5 Caledonian Road, London N1 (01-837 7324)

Gingerbread 35 Wellington Street, London WC2 (01-240 0953); association of single parent families.

Grapevine, 296 Holloway Road, London N7 (01-607 0949; advice answer phone 01-607 0935); free advice and support on sex and personal problems.

Health Education Council 78 New Oxford Street, London WC1 (01-637 1881); free leaflets on sexual development, VD, drugs, contraception etc.

Howard League for Penal Reform 125 Kennington Park Road, London SE11 (01-735 3773)

International Adoption Society, 160 Peckham Rye, London SE22 (01-693 9611); counselling for single pregnant girls.

International Social Service 39 Brixton Road, London SW9 (01-735 8941); can advise on marriage to a citizen of a foreign country

Irish Centre 52 Camden Square, London NW1 (01-485 0051); advice and practical help for Irish people in London

Justice Against Identification Laws (JAIL) 271 Upper Street London N1 (01-359 8034)

Joint Council for the Welfare of Immigrants 44 Theobalds Road, London WC1 (01-405 5527); advice and help on immigration and citizenship problems

Legal Action Group, 28A Highgate Road, London NW5 (01-485 1189); can provide list of local law centres

Martin Luther King Memorial Trust 1-3 Hildreth Street, London SW12 (01-673 6511); concerned with black youth

National Abortion Campaign 374 Grays Inn Road, London WC1 (01-278 0153)

National Association for the Care and Resettlement of Offenders 125 Kennington Park Road, London SE11 (01-735 1151)

National Association for Mental Health (MIND) 22 Harley Street, London W1 (01-637 0741)

National Council for Civil Liberties 186 Kings Cross Road, London WC1 (01-278 4575); campaigning organisation, can also advise on sex and race discrimination, police powers, prisoners' rights etc.

National Council for One Parent Families 255 Kentish Town Road, London NW5 (01-267 1361)

National Marriage Guidance Council Herbert College, Little Church Street, Rugby (0788-73241; look in local phone book or contact them for local number); helps couples aged 16 or over, married or not.

National Society for the Prevention of Cruelty to Children 1 Riding House Street, London W1 (01-580 8812)

National Union of Students and National Union of School Students 302 Pentonville Road, London N1 (01-278 3291) (temporary address); 3 Endsleigh Street, London WC1 (01-387 1277)

National Women's Aid Federation 374 Grays Inn Road, London WC1 (01-837 9316)

Northern Ireland Civil Rights Association 2 Marquis Street, Belfast (0232 23351)

Radical Alternatives to Prison 104A Brackenbury Road, London W6 (01-748 5778)

Release 1 Elgin Avenue, London W9 (01-289 1123; out of office hours 01-603 8654); advice on drugs, abortion, police powers and the courts etc; can refer you to a solicitor.

Rights of Women 374 Grays Inn Road, London WC1 (01-278 6349); legal advice on women's rights

Royal Scottish Corporation 37 King Street, London WC2 (01-240 3718); advice and help for Scots people in London.

Samaritans (London 01-626 2277; look in phone book for local numbers); help the suicidal.

111

Schools Council 160 Great Portland Street, London W1 (01-580 0352)

Scottish Association for the Care and Resettlement of Offenders 110 West Bow, Edinburgh (031-225 5232)

Scottish Child Poverty Action Group 70 Nicholson Street, Edinburgh (031-667 0415)

Scottish Council for Civil Liberties (SCCL) 146 Holland Street, Glasgow G1 (041-332 5960)

Scottish Council for Single Parents 44 Albany Street, Edinburgh EH1 (031-556 3899)

Shelter Housing Aid Centre 189a Old Brompton Road, London SW5 (01-373 7276)

Shelter 157 Waterloo Road, London SE1 (01-633 9377)

Society of Teachers Opposed to Physical Punishment (STOPP) 10 Lennox Gardens, Croydon, Surrey CR0 4HR

Trades Union Congress (TUC) Congress House, 23-8 Great Russell Street, London WC1 (01-636 4030)

Ulster Pregnancy Advisory Service 338 Lisburn Road, Belfast 9 (0232-667345)

United Kingdom Immigrants Advisory Service 7th floor, Brettenham House, Savoy Street, London WC2 (01-240 5176); advice and help on immigration, citizenship and refugee problems